T0194288

Free
SPIRIT

Rediscovering Your God-Given Identity

CHARLES CAVIOLA

WESTBOW
P R E S S®
A DIVISION OF THOMAS NELSON
& ZONDERVAN

Scripture quotations are taken from THE HOLY BIBLE, NEW
INTERNATIONAL VERSION®, NIV® Copyright © 1973, 1978, 1984,
2011 by Biblica, Inc.® Used by permission. All rights reserved worldwide.

WestBow Press books may be ordered through
booksellers or by contacting:

WestBow Press
A Division of Thomas Nelson & Zondervan
1663 Liberty Drive
Bloomington, IN 47403
www.westbowpress.com
1 (866) 928-1240

ISBN: 978-1-9736-5126-0 (sc)
ISBN: 978-1-9736-5127-7 (e)

Print information available on the last page.

WestBow Press rev. date: 01/22/2019

CONTENTS

INTRODUCTION

I look around and I see a world that is having a major identity crisis. I'm not just talking about from a faith or religious observation (I will get to that in a moment), but from a social, cultural, and moral position. People for the most part seem to have an issue figuring out or knowing who they are.

The world can be a very convincing place, with the influence of media and celebrity personalities that command the attention and allegiance of their viewers and fans it's no wonder why people are trying to be someone or something that they are not. As I ponder some of the issues that society is facing on a daily basis I wonder what changed. I wonder if at some point people became more willing to accept the views and advice of someone who carries with them a certain level of celebrity and stopped taking the advice of the God who created them. It's another form of manipulation and deception it's just that it's no longer a serpent in the garden, it's a celebrity on a T.V. screen or a teacher in a classroom.

We have been steered so far in the wrong direction as a people and a culture that we no longer desire to listen to or do what is right, we do what feels good. We have bought this line "if being wrong feels this good, I don't want to be right". We don't care about the consequences of the choices that we make, but we don't like it when we are told that we are wrong. We have adopted a political correctness and divorced truth and reason, the apostle Paul says in 1 Corinthians 10:23 *"I have the right to do anything, you say-but not everything is beneficial."* So where do we stop living for the "feels" and start living for the truth? when do we stop listening to what every celebrity and fallible person has to say about us and start listening to the truth of the Word of the God who made us?

I have been given a passion as a result of seeing people set free from false identity and brought into the freedom of the truth of who they were made to be by God. I have seen the torment of those who have allowed the lies of society and the misguided information of the world to form and manipulate who they are. It is time that people hear the truth that God made you fearfully and wonderfully, that you are not an accident, mistake, failure, unloved, undesirable, or unimportant. You are none of those things, God made you because He loves you and He wants you to have a full life. God doesn't make mistakes, and He certainly didn't make one when He made you, He made a masterpiece.

CHAPTER
ONE

WHERE IT ALL BEGINS

Genesis 1:27-31New International Version (NIV)
²⁷ So God created mankind in his own image,
in the image of God he created them;
male and female he created them.

²⁸ God blessed them and said to them, "Be
fruitful and increase in number; fill the earth and
subdue it. Rule over the fish in the sea and the
birds in the sky and over every living creature that
moves on the ground."

²⁹ Then God said, "I give you every seed-bearing
plant on the face of the whole earth and every tree
that has fruit with seed in it. They will be yours
for food. ³⁰ And to all the beasts of the earth and
all the birds in the sky and all the creatures that
move along the ground—everything that has the

breath of life in it—I give every green plant for food." And it was so.

³¹ God saw all that he had made, and it was very good. And there was evening, and there was morning—the sixth day.

1. What are four key points that we take away regarding identity when we read this passage?
   - We were created in the IMAGE of God.

What does that look like to you? If I asked to to reflect on what you think the image of God looks like would you say that you reflect that image? Now I can imagine what you're saying "it's impossible to fully reflect God" and in some ways I may agree with you, but didn't Jesus in HIs full humanity show us what it was like to be the reflection of our heavenly Father? Although Jesus was fully divine at the same time the Word of God says:

Philippians 2:6-8 New International Version (NIV)

> **6** *Who, being in very nature God, did not consider equality with God something to be used to his own advantage;* **7** *rather, he made himself nothing by taking the very nature of a servant, being made in human likeness.***8** *And being found in appearance as a man, he humbled himself by becoming obedient to death—even death on a cross!*

> Jesus was the model for man what it was like to emulate and reflect the presence of God. So again I ask, What does it look like

to reflect the character of God if we were
created in His image?
-    We were created BLESSED.

What does this look like? I heard this quote that is simple
yet profound, it goes like this…" we are called to fight from
victory, not for victory". I can insert some words here to
drive my point, "we are called to live from blessing, not
for blessing" When we keep asking God for blessings that
means that we feel as though we aren't already blessed…
sometimes. What if we shifted our understanding of how
we were created by realizing that God has already made His
blessings for us accessible and available and all we have to do
is start seeing the blessings happening throughout our lives.
Oftentimes our worldview of how we perceive blessings is
tainted by our culture and society. Blessed is subject to our
financial status, marital status, job status, popularity, and
social status. God's idea of blessing is not subject to worldly
things, rather it is found in the understanding that God loves
you so much that He has plans and purposes for your life
that are non perishable, and that when we live in those plans
and purposes then all the other things that we need in our
lives fall into place.

Matthew 6:28-33 New International Version (NIV)

28 *"And why do you worry about clothes? See how the flowers of
the field grow. They do not labor or spin.* **29** *Yet I tell you that not
even Solomon in all his splendor was dressed like one of these.* **30**
*If that is how God clothes the grass of the field, which is here today
and tomorrow is thrown into the fire, will he not much more clothe
you—you of little faith?* **31** *So do not worry, saying, 'What shall
we eat?' or 'What shall we drink?' or 'What shall we wear?'* **32**

For the pagans run after all these things, and your heavenly Father knows that you need them. 33 But seek first his kingdom and his righteousness, and all these things will be given to you as well.

- We were created with and in authority.

The Kingdom of God is not powerless, therefor if our manufacturer is powerful He gives us power as well. We must understand something in regards to the theology of the two gardens. In the beginning God bestowed authority to man and women that they might have dominion over all living creatures and the land. When they made agreement with the serpent who had no authority, they forfeited what God gave them to Satan. It was in the Garden where Jesus was tempted that the authority was won back and made available again to the followers of Christ. This authority was displayed by Christ for the purpose of teaching all believers that they too possess the same authority. In Acts 16 we see a demonstration of this authority when Paul and Silas were being "harassed" by a slave girl that the Bible says had a spirit. The way that this situation played out was so matter of fact and organic that it has to be a perfect display of an identity that lives in full authority. Paul turned around and **COMMANDED** the spirit to come out of her. The Word of God is filled with emphatic commands that defy human limitation by stepping into a heavenly authority. When we live in the authority that we are created in, people are healed, demons flee, and death is overcome in the name of Jesus because there is power in the name of Jesus.

Matthew 10:1-8 New International Version (NIV) Jesus Sends Out the Twelve

10 *Jesus called his twelve disciples to him and gave them authority to drive out impure spirits and to heal every disease and sickness.*

2 *These are the names of the twelve apostles: first, Simon (who is called Peter) and his brother Andrew; James son of Zebedee, and his brother John;* **3** *Philip and Bartholomew; Thomas and Matthew the tax collector; James son of Al phaeus, and Thaddaeus;* **4** *Simon the Zealot and Judas Iscariot, who betrayed him.*

5 *These twelve Jesus sent out with the following instructions: "Do not go among the Gentiles or enter any town of the Samaritans.* **6** *Go rather to the lost sheep of Israel.* **7** *As you go, proclaim this message: 'The kingdom of heaven has come near.'* **8** *Heal the sick, raise the dead, cleanse those who have leprosy,[a] drive out demons. Freely you have received; freely give.*

- We were created good
What does it mean to be a GOOD creation?

In the beginning God gave all authority to man, we had the ability and opportunity to have control over all things that lived on the earth. We were truly co laborers with God and were heirs to the kingdom. In chapter 3 of Genesis we experience the fall of man which lead to the forfeiting of the authority that God gave us to satan. This fall lead to three big issues.

1. We entered into a broken relationship with God when we were created to have relationship with Him.
2. We forfeited our authority when we were given all authority.
3. Sin and death entered our reality.

When this occurred, the enemy entered into the body of Christ with the purpose of blinding it's followers to the truth of the Gospel which robs people of the authority that we receive at conversion, and continually separates us from God.

We adopt the image of the world and forfeit the image of God. The image of the world is:

1. Idolatry: We place worldly figures on a pedestal and minimize our need to connect with God.
2. Greed: We strive to obtain things that take place of the gifts that God has for us. We desire more money, more friends, more material possession. This ultimately becomes our primary focus and what we worship.
3. Alternative identity: we desire to be like everyone else when God made us to stand apart from everyone else

Psalm 139:14New International Version (NIV)
¹⁴ I praise you because I am fearfully and
wonderfully made;
your works are wonderful,
I know that full well.

This Psalm stands in direct opposition with the image that the world paints of who we are. The interpretation of this Psalm from its original language tells us that we were created in a way that is beyond explanation or intellectual reason.

So if the world can't explain us, why do we allow it the authority to define us?

We forfeit our blessings for mediocrity.

In the Old Testament whenever a young man was blessed by his father, it was a very profound and significant moment. The blessing from a father brought a spiritual impartation which released Kingdom destinies. The blessing of the father would almost be like a key unlocking a storehouse filled with treasure.

Gen 17:15-17 gives us the account of Isaac receiving a blessing from his father because of his father's faithfulness to God.

Gen 25 we read about Jacob taking the blessing from his father which unlocked bountiful blessing and the creation of the nation of Israel.

The beatitudes that Jesus taught from the mountain speak of what blessings come through, faithful obedience from our Father in Heaven. There is no such thing as a mediocre blessing, but we often times accept crumbs ignoring the feast that has been displayed before us. Our blessings are not just things that are physical, although it does not exclude them. Our Blessings are other worldly and therefore reveal a heavenly reality.

When we look at blessings that occur in scripture, none of them are blessings that man is capable of creating in his own power, the blessings that occur point to the majesty of God and His kingdom.

We forfeit our authority and accept the weaker alternative.

Our authority is standing in agreement with the promises that God has spoken through His Word. We are told that we are heirs to a Holy kingdom, meaning that we have direct access to the storehouses of heaven when we stand in agreement with the will of God.

A person who lives with that authority looks like an earthly rule breaker because by all worldly explanation they shouldn't be able to accomplish the things that will be manifested through them.

When Adam and Eve ate from the tree, they stood in defiance to God and questioned His Word. When we stand in opposition or don't take God at His word, then we are in disagreement and will live a powerless life of worldly enslavement.

We no longer see good.

Our eyes become unfocused, they see all of the effects of the fall happening all around them, but they fail to see the beauty of God working in the midst of it. It is Satan's greatest victory that we take our eyes off of the good that is happening all around us and gets us fully focused on the troubles that we face in life.

One of the most dangerous things that we can do that steers our identity in a misguided direction is to make agreement with the lies about who we are. The enemy who comes to lie, steal, kill, and destroy wants you to believe that you are something that you are not. He will do anything that he can to persuade you to believe the lies. So how do we break out of the lies and the darkness and into the truth where there is light and life? if you have agreed with the lies about anything (you're a failure, unlovable, stupid, ugly, weak) whatever it may be, you made a covenant with him. First you need to start by repenting to God for allowing the lies to define you when God is the one who should be defining you. Second, ask the Lord to restore you to your true identity, just ask Him to bring fresh revelation of His original intent and plan for you. Sometimes we get so tired in life that we will accept anything that gives us a definition for who we are or why we are the way we are, when in reality it's deception. Remember when Jesus was in His hometown of Nazareth and the people said "Isn't this Jesus the son of Joseph the carpenter"? what they were doing was diminishing His identity. Yes He was Jesus the son of Joseph the carpenter, but He was so much more that that. And the people missed the fullness of who He was because they were not able to see beyond the tangible physical stuff. When people see us they might just see who we are according to our worldly titles or positions, but we have a name that is greater than what the world can place on us and a title that is held higher than any worldly position can handle.

YOU ARE A TESTIMONY

Throughout scripture, we read accounts of how God transformed people from men and women who lived lives that did not reflect and glorify God, to becoming people who were incarnational carriers of His presence and power.

Hebrews 10:32-36 New International Version (NIV)

[32] Remember those earlier days after you had received the light, when you endured in a great conflict full of suffering. [33] Sometimes you were publicly exposed to insult and persecution; at other times you stood side by side with those who were so treated. [34] You suffered along with those in prison and joyfully accepted the confiscation of your property, because you knew that you yourselves had better and lasting possessions. [35] So do not throw away your confidence; it will be richly rewarded.

[36] You need to persevere so that when you have done the will of God, you will receive what he has promised.

The writer to the Hebrews is exhorting the readers to remember where the Lord has brought them. From a life of empty religion to a life of faith and salvation. This is a redemptive process that brought the people of God from a time of slavery and alienation in their own land to a place of sonship.

I think of the Apostle Paul, formerly Saul, a murderous man determined to kill as many Christians as possible is miraculously transformed by the power of Jesus Christ and changed forever. When you read throughout the New testament letters of Paul you see that he is constantly reminding people of who he was and who he is now.

1 Timothy 1:15-17 New International Version (NIV)

15 *Here is a trustworthy saying that deserves full acceptance: Christ Jesus came into the world to save sinners—of whom I am the worst.* **16** *But for that very reason I was shown mercy so that in me, the worst of sinners, Christ Jesus might display his immense patience as an example for those who would believe in him and receive eternal life.* **17** *Now to the King eternal, immortal, invisible, the only God, be honor and glory for ever and ever. Amen.*

A testimony is not just a story for others to know about us that they may hear about the work of God in our lives, but it is also to serve as a reminder to us that when we face times in our lives that challenge our faith, we rest upon the testimony of when God reached into our lives and called us to something greater. One of my mentors said to me "no one can take your testimony" meaning if you had an encounter with Christ, their acceptance of your testimony or not has no leanings on the validity of your experience.

Through the process of recording some of the events in our lives, we can see where we have gone wrong, and we can see where God was present when we didn't think He was even there. I have experienced both when I went through my testimony, I saw the things that I allowed into my life that shaped some of my identity and decisions, and I saw God in the places where I felt my loneliest. I have learned to not let my mistakes shape or define me, rather I found the courage to let God reshape and correct me in those places. The result for me was absolutely freeing, I felt like me again and I no longer felt as though I was living in a haze of confusion.

What is your testimony?

I invite you to take a day or two to reflect on your testimony. What God moments have you had in your life that either brought you to faith or deepened your faith? This is an exercise in mapping out your life and seeing all of the moments where God showed up. It's a praise letter that glorifies God in your life and encourages you because you will see even in some moments that seemed hopeless or when you felt that God wasn't even there that there was hope and that God was present.

Psalm 71:15-18 New International Version (NIV)

> **15** *My mouth will tell of your righteous deeds, of your saving acts all day long— though I know not how to relate them all.*
>
> **16** *I will come and proclaim your mighty acts, Sovereign Lord; I will proclaim your righteous deeds, yours alone.*
>
> **17** *Since my youth, God, you have taught me, and to this day I declare your marvelous deeds.*
>
> **18** *Even when I am old and gray, do not forsake me, my God, till I declare your power to the next generation, your mighty acts to all who are to come.*

WHY GOD MADE YOU

Isaiah 43:7New International Version (NIV)
[7] everyone who is called by my name,
whom I created for my glory,
whom I formed and made."

We are made for His glory.

The word in Hebrew is *Kabod* which translates as *Glorious Splendor*. The translation of this word connotes a reflection of the identity of the one whom you are to imitate. It is an identity that brings honor to God through the way that you live your life. Jesus lead the example of glorifying God with your life, He came against a life that sought fame from the world by doing things that glorified self and drew the attention and accolade of man. Everything that He taught was to give glory to God.

In short you were created to reflect the character and presence of God Himself.

Ephesians 3:9-10 New International Version (NIV)

[9] and to make plain to everyone the administration of this mystery, which for ages past was kept hidden in God, who created all things. [10] His intent was that now, through the church, the manifold wisdom of God should be made known to the rulers and authorities in the heavenly realms,

We were made to reveal heavens plan.

Through the life that we lead Paul tells us that we are to illuminate people's understanding of the great mystery of salvation that rests in Christ. We are called to be people who reveal the gift of salvation to those who are perishing, this calls us to connect the calling of the great commission with our identity. The great commission calls us to go out and do, our identity calls us to go out and be.

As miracles ourselves we are to live in a way that is outside of intellectual explanation and to be a reflection of the "mystery". It is part of our testimony that we have first received the saving Grace from God and secondly that we are now living transformed lives that deny worldly power or authority.

1 Corinthians 15:27-28New International Version (NIV)

[27] For he "has put everything under his feet." Now when it says that "everything" has been put under him, it is clear that this does not include God himself, who put everything under Christ. [28] When he has done this, then the Son himself will be made subject to him who put everything under him, so that God may be all in all.

We were made to represent His authority.

This may be a confusing passage of scripture, but the gist of it states that God gave all authority to Christ, who when He ascended after conquering the principalities of hell and earth returned those keys of authority to God the father.

Now that Christ serves as an intermediary between us and the Father and whatever we ask for in the name of Jesus will be done because He makes petition for us to the Father, we share the authority with God. It is an agreement policy that when we ask Him for the purpose of reflecting His will, then we see the manifest presence of God operating in our midst.

The "everything" that Paul speaks of is all occurrences that happen in the physical realm, when Jesus walked this earth in the full authority of God, all of those things i.e. Sickness, death, demonic powers etc. where subject to that very authority. We have been called back to an authority in Christ to make those things subject to the presence of Christ in us.

John 14:12New International Version (NIV)

12 Very truly I tell you, whoever believes in me will do the works I have been doing, and they will do even greater things than these, because I am going to the Father.

When Jesus spoke these words, He was passing the proverbial torch to His followers. The fact that Jesus spoke these words telling the disciples that everything that they had seen Him accomplish right before their very eyes (healings, miracles, deliverance, dead being raised etc.) will also be done by them in greater volume and capacity because they have a divine resource to tap into. This passage of the passing on of authority goes hand in hand with the mandate that we read in Matthew 10:

Matthew 10:8New International Version (NIV)

8 Heal the sick, raise the dead, cleanse those who have leprosy, drive out demons. Freely you have received; freely give.

In essence, it would be fitting to say that we are created to be available vessels to be filled with the presence of God and clothed in His Holy Spirit to be a manifestation of all that He truly represents. When we cast off the identity of the flesh and the world, then we step into a heavenly garment which reflects the glory of God.

WHY GOD CHOSE YOU

Ephesians 1:4New International Version (NIV)

⁴ For he chose us in him before the creation of the world to be holy and blameless in his sight. In love

God wants you to be the best version of you that you can be! To be Holy is a pursuit that we enter into with God to become more like Him. By definition to be Holy means to be perfect in goodness and righteousness. On our own and by our own efforts we will fall short of this pursuit since we live in an imperfect world, but in Christ we are made for more than to just be products of an imperfect world, but to be a product of a perfect God.

To be chosen in Him speaks of the relational longing that God has for us. That He desires a uniting of us to Him. He chose you for relationship, He chose you so that you can know His love.

1 Peter 2:9New International Version (NIV)

⁹ But you are a chosen people, a royal priesthood, a holy nation, God's special possession, that you may declare the praises of him who called you out of darkness into his wonderful light.

God chose us to be participants in His divine plan. He desires for us to operate in a heavenly office here on earth. In the same way that kingdoms and monarchies throughout history chose the heir to the throne, God has chosen you and me to be co heirs to a heavenly kingdom, but the difference is that we are ambassadors called to impart heavenly authority here on earth. Everyone knows a King when they are face to face with one, they look like a King, they talk like a King, they rule like a King. We are to look like God's workmanship, talk like God's workmanship, and rule like God's workmanship.

John 15:16New International Version (NIV)

16 You did not choose me, but I chose you and appointed you so that you might go and bear fruit—fruit that will last—and so that whatever you ask in my name the Father will give you.

He chose you so that He can give you good things so that your life would reflect the goodness of Him who gave you those gifts.

Workshop moment:

Enter into a time of praise thanking God that He chose us, that He anoints us, that He gives us good gifts, but more than anything, that He created us to love us. There are prayer teams available to pray an impartation of the identity of son ship that you may know that you were created special and set apart for a unique and divine purpose.

Final note:

You were created for more! The Word of God tells us in Romans 8:37 that we are more than conquerors. This would lead me to believe that we are more than average, mediocrity wasn't in the blueprint when God designed and called you. If we serve a God who is capable of so much, then why would we settle for anything less than what He has to fully offer?

An identity that stops short of the full image that God has of us is a powerless and unfulfilled identity. When we step into the fullness of a God filled identity we will experience what the Church is really supposed to look like which is a gathering of sold out followers of Jesus hungry for greater intimacy with the Father and desiring greater partnership with the Holy Spirit.

Workshop moment:

What the world says about you and what the Word says about you tend to be completely contradictory. Have you adopted a false identity from the world? have you allowed the world or society to sell you a lie? Ask the Holy Spirit to reveal to you anything that you have accepted that isn't from the Lord and give Him permission to shatter it and reveal the truth of who you are.

TWO

HOW TO KNOW GOD

"The healthy Christian is not necessarily the extrovert, ebullient Christian, but the Christian who has a sense of God's presence stamped deep on his soul, who trembles at God's word, who lets it dwell in him richly by constant meditation upon it, and who tests and reforms his life daily in response to it."

J.I. Packer <u>A quest for Godliness</u>, p. 116

I am one hundred percent certain that if you went to one hundred Churches around the country and asked people if they know God, they would say yes, but then if you asked them to describe God they would use a plethora of Bible knowledge that they gained from the multiple Bible studies that they have attended which describe the character and being of God. Now this isn't a bad thing, but it's not the goal of the Christian, the goal is to know God on an intimate level. When the Bible talks about knowing God, it uses two words, in the Hebrew it uses the word *yada* and in the greek it uses the word *ginosko* both words are defined as a relational knowing like you know your spouse or a close friend. Sadly enough if you asked those people in those one hundred Churches, the majority would probably not know what it is like to intimately know God.

Jeremiah 9:23-24New International Version (NIV)

[23] This is what the LORD says: "Let not the wise boast of their wisdom
or the strong boast of their strength
or the rich boast of their riches,
[24] but let the one who boasts boast about this:
that they have the understanding to know me,
that I am the LORD, who exercises kindness,
justice and righteousness on earth,
for in these I delight,"
declares the LORD.

So how do we get to **KNOW** God?

1. Intimacy
   - Make your own tent of meeting: Moses in Gen 33 during the wanderings had his own tent which he would enter to meet with the Lord. It says that when Moses entered he would meet with God face to face. It was during this time of meeting that Moses would learn more about who God is on an intimate level. Because of this time that Moses would spend with God, he would be given a renewed purpose. When we enter into the presence, we want to remain there, but when we walk out of our meeting we

go with the power and presence of God. When we experience Him on new levels, we become hungrier for His presence.

- Ask God to search you: Spending time in the presence of God through time of quiet prayer and meditation is key to knowing God in a deeper way. In Psalm 139 David became transparent before the Lord, he asked that God would search him so that he might have a deeper knowledge of God's plan, purpose, and love for him.

- Be surrendered: When we go before the Lord, we have to be ready and expectant that He may ask something of us that will challenge us. Samuel before he knew the Lord heard from Him as He spoke to gain Samuels attention. Again Samuel like Moses was in a posture that was willing to hear and receive from the Lord. He heard Him in the stillness and was tasked with a great responsibility to be the prophet over Israel. But Samuel wanted it! he wanted to hear from God and he did.

- He has to be first: We need to make His presence, His voice, His love more important than the very air we breathe. If we put Him second then I can't imagine that He will go out of HIs way to meet us. We have to have a heart the runs to His presence, that is eager to hear His voice, and is desperate to feel His heart. The famous song by Annie S. Hawks recites *"I

need thee, Oh I need thee, every hour I need thee,
bless me know, my savior, I come to thee". That is
a desperation for the presence of God that begs
Him to speak for your servant is listening.

2.   Behold Him

Proverbs 2:1-5New International Version (NIV)

Moral Benefits of Wisdom

2 *My son, if you accept my words*
   and store up my commands within you,
[2] *turning your ear to wisdom*
   and applying your heart to understanding—
[3] *indeed, if you call out for insight*
   and cry aloud for understanding,
[4] *and if you look for it as for silver*
   and search for it as for hidden treasure,
[5] *then you will understand the fear of the* LORD
   and find the knowledge of God.

-    Listen to Him: The discipline of listening
     to the Lord is one of complete humility and
     surrender. When we listen to the Lord we are
     telling Him that He is worthy of our attention.
     By reading the Word of God we are allowing
     our minds to perceive what is truth, but by
     turning our hearts to a posture of listening
     to what the Lord is wanting us to hear in the
     Spirit we can comprehend the reality of His
     being. John 1 tells us that in the beginning the
     Word was with God and was God and that the

Word became flesh. When we stop treating the Word as simply what is written in the pages of scripture and start treating it as a physical living and breathing being, then we come into contact and relationship with God Himself.

Deuteronomy 28:1-2New International Version (NIV)

Blessings for Obedience

28 *If you fully obey the L*ORD *your God and carefully follow all his commands I give you today, the L*ORD *your God will set you high above all the nations on earth. ² All these blessings will come on you and accompany you if you obey the L*ORD *your God:*

- Obey Him: When we take the time to listen to the voice of God speaking to us, then we experience the outpouring of His Glory. When we behold all that the Lord is, then we will be filled with a desire to submit to His commands. When we do this, then we will know His goodness.

3. Gaze upon Him

   "How can we turn our knowledge about God into knowledge of God? The rule for doing this is simple but demanding. It is that we turn each Truth that we learn about God into matter for meditation before God, leading to prayer and praise to God."
   – J.I. Packer, *Knowing God* p.23

In Psalm 119, David writes over and over again about the benefits of meditating on the Lord and His Word. What we gain from reading this section of scripture is that meditation is a discipline which allows God to reveal things to our Spirit. The act of gazing upon the Lord draws us to a place where we don't just listen, but we fully comprehend by hearing Him.

When we meditate we go inward, where the Holy Spirit of God dwells in the believer. There we make personal intercession for our very souls that we would petition God to enlighten us to see things in deeper more illumined ways. It is the secret place that unfolds the very character and being of God, this place requires us to shut off the world and to take a seat in an otherworldly place where distractions are put aside so that we can hear clearly from the Lord as He engages with us.

Workshop moment:

I think it's time for another workshop moment. This time I want you to go to a quiet place. Go ahead, find the best place in the house to get away from distraction and just be in the silence. Take three deep slow breaths, and ask the Lord to come. Ask Him to invade your space and overwhelm you with His presence. When you feel Him in the room give Him thanks. This is a time for you to just let God love on you for a bit. When you feel like you can come out of that space, write down what you felt God doing. A good reminder is great medicine for the times when we need a quick shot of the love of Jesus.

HOW TO KNOW THE HOLY SPIRIT

When I think about the Holy Spirit I think of a Wild horse, it is absolutely beautiful, filled with awe and wonder, you can gaze upon its beauty and absolute power but must realize that it isn't something to be controlled or broken. The Holy Spirit is something that the Church has seemingly in many ways attempted to domesticate and has only then succeeded in sterilizing it. The Holy Spirit must be treated as someone to cooperate with, when we befriend the third person of the trinity then we can take part in enjoying it's company and benefit from His qualities.

The Church in many ways seeks to know the Holy Spirit through intellectual reasoning, it denies true Holy Spirit activity passing it off as human impossibility not realizing that the Holy Spirit works beyond our mere human understanding and operates on a supernatural scale.

"It is quite plain in the scriptural revelation that spiritual things are hidden by a veil, and by nature a human does not have the ability to comprehend and get a hold of them. He comes up against a blank wall. He takes doctrine and texts and proofs and creeds and theology, and lays them up like a wall but he cannot find the

gate! He stands in the darkness and all about him is intellectual knowledge of God but not the true knowledge of God, for there is a difference between the intellectual knowledge of God and the Spirit revealed knowledge". - A.W. Tozer, *The Counselor p.18*

1. Let Him guide your understanding of who He is. Sometimes when we get caught up in our temporal mind, then we end up explaining away so many of the mysteries of the Word of God. One of the characteristics of the Holy Spirit is that He guides us to a deeper understanding of the Word of God and brings an enlightenment to deeper things.

John 16:12-13New International Version (NIV)
12 "I have much more to say to you, more than you can now bear. 13 But when he, the Spirit of truth, comes, he will guide you into all the truth. He will not speak on his own; he will speak only what he hears, and he will tell you what is yet to come.

In this passage of scripture Jesus is telling the disciples that there are deep truths and revelations that will come to them through the enlightenment of the Holy Spirit. Notice where Jesus says that He has much more to say to us, more than we can bear. What He is telling us is that our intellectual minds will never be able to comprehend the depth of what He wants to show us so therefore it can only be fully realized through the unfolding of its mystery by the Holy Spirit. Spiritual understanding and revelation far outweigh the value of the intellect when it comes to knowing the Holy Spirit.

John 14:26New International Version (NIV)

²⁶ But the Advocate, the Holy Spirit, whom the Father will send in my name, will teach you all things and will remind you of everything I have said to you.

2. Set your mind on Him. When we think with a worldly mind that is controlled by the events and outcomes of our daily lives, then we are not allowing ourselves to be controlled by the Spirit of God.

One of the movies that I loved it the Matrix, the baseline of the movie is Neo this average guy working in an office grinding it away from nine to five is unbeknownst to him the chosen one. One day he meets a man named Morpheus who grants Neo the opportunity to step into his destiny by taking a red pill, or to stay in his normal way of life by taking the blue pill. The red pill will open up Neo's mind to a reality that exists outside of the human understanding, it will enlighten him to the under workings of the world that he knows. I like to look at the Holy Spirit as taking the red pill, when we allow Him to come and transform our minds and the way that we observe things in this world, then we will enter into a reality that is purely spiritual and part temporal.

Romans 8:5New International Version (NIV)
⁵ Those who live according to the flesh have their minds set on what the flesh desires; but those who live in accordance with the Spirit have their minds set on what the Spirit desires.

In this life, in the reality that we perceive with our five senses, we observe everything from a fleshly viewpoint. When you sin, it was simply a slip up, a momentary temptation that grabbed a hold of you. But when you are living a life that is controlled by the Spirit, then we see that it wasn't just happenstance that this happened, but that there was a spiritual catalyst behind the fall. Coincidences don't exist when we live a life that is controlled by the Spirit, we see God's hand in all things. Whether they be tragedy, triumph, healing, or trials, when we understand the spiritual involvement in the things of this life them we will engage them on a spiritual level.

Galatians 5:16-18New International Version (NIV)
¹⁶ So I say, walk by the Spirit, and you will not gratify the desires of the flesh.¹⁷ For the flesh desires what is contrary to the Spirit, and the Spirit what is contrary to the flesh. They are in conflict with each other, so that you are not to do whatever you want. ¹⁸ But if you are led by the Spirit, you are not under the law.

3. Let Him fall upon you. When we accept Jesus Christ as our Lord and savior, we receive the deposit of the Holy Spirit within us. But what we don't always acknowledge is the element of the Holy Spirit upon us. If the Holy Spirit within us is a seal upon our hearts marking us as saved, then the Holy Spirit upon us is a seal of God's power.

Acts 1:8New International Version (NIV)
⁸ But you will receive power when the Holy Spirit comes on you; and you will be my witnesses in Jerusalem, and in all Judea and Samaria, and to the ends of the earth."

HOW TO ENGAGE GOD

Micah 6:6-8New International Version (NIV)
⁶ With what shall I come before the LORD and
bow down before the exalted God?
Shall I come before him with burnt
offerings, with calves a year old?
⁷ Will the LORD be pleased with thousands of
rams, with ten thousand rivers of olive oil?
Shall I offer my firstborn for my transgression, the
fruit of my body for the sin of my soul?
⁸ He has shown you, O mortal, what is good.
And what does the LORD require of you?
To act justly and to love mercy and to
walk humbly with your God.

In the military they call it R.O.E or Rules of Engagement. It is the guidelines that all soldiers are called to follow while in combat. In our faith we also have Rules of Engagement but the difference is that these rules start from a place of surrender.

Let's paint a scenario.......let's say that one day you received an invitation to attend a banquet where you would have the opportunity to meet a King. Customarily the protocol would be that you would attend this event with a gift that you would present to this royal figure as a sign of appreciation for the King's service. You would of course want to present the King with the best gift that you could afford. The thought and the cost that you put into the gift that you present would be indicative or your loyalty to that King.

This is also the way that we approach God. In the Old Testament when the people wanted to engage God, they would customarily present offerings. The rams and the olive oil would have been items of great value, they would have been a sacrifice. When we approach God, do we offer Him the best of ourselves, or do we offer Him a meager portion?

Isaiah 6:8New International Version (NIV)
⁸ Then I heard the voice of the Lord saying, "Whom shall I send? And who will go for us?"
And I said, "Here am I. Send me!"

We Engage God in our offering, in the way that we present ourselves as a willing sacrifice to be used according to His will. When we engage God on a personal level we can't help but to enter into it His will with a heart of servitude to our King. When we do this we must be ready and willing to respond in a fashion that will please the King. When Isaiah heard this voice posing the question who shall I send? He was in a place of availability. He was in a place where he was "out of the world, and into the heavenly" he positioned himself in a place of prayer, reflection, and meditation on the presence of the Lord expecting that God was going to speak to him.

Workshop moment:

Let's take 15-20 minutes at this point to be present for the Lord, while we are in this place of stillness let's ask God to meet with us so that we may engage Him on a personal level. During this time of stillness I would encourage you to journal what you sense the Lord saying to you.

Holy Spirit come, invade this space that i dwell in and come and speak to me. I hunger for your voice Lord and desire to hear you speak. Open my ears to hear you and remove all earthly distractions and still my mind that I may focus on what you want to say to me. Speak Lord your servant is listening.

HOW TO COOPERATE WITH THE HOLY SPIRIT

The Holy Spirit is like what some people might identify as a conscience, let me explain. It is the inward nudging that draws us to a recollection of right and wrong, of impending danger like a sixth sense, and enlightens us to certain truths. But the Holy Spirit most of all draws us to intimacy with God.

The Holy Spirit is working within the heart of every believer, that upon a profession of faith they are immediately infused with His presence. This presence draws us to a hunger and desire for relationship with God and a reconnection with Him while in sin. When we sin, and we feel that sense deep in the pit of our soul that we have acted in a morally depraved way, the Holy Spirit draws us back to the Father through repentance. I think that one way that we deny cooperating with the Holy Spirit would to live in disunity from God.

I have heard it spoken of as a dance, cooperating with the Holy Spirit is likened to as a beautiful dance where the partners are in perfect sync and timing with one another. I am not a naturally good dancer, my wife will attest to that fact. When I dance my timing and my rhythm are not necessarily spot on, I fear many times that because I am not in sync with my wife I might step on her toes, or trip her up. We can do the same with the Holy Spirit if we aren't in sync with him, it requires discipline and attention. If we are in the sweet spot with the Holy Spirit then we are in unity with the Father and therefore we will be available to engage Him in a way that is supernatural.

The Holy Spirit guides us in prayer and contemplation

Jude 20 New international version (NIV)
But you, dear friends, build yourselves up in your most holy faith and pray in the Holy spirit.
Ephesians 6:18 New international version (NIV)
And pray in the spirit on all occasions with all kinds of prayers and requests.

Prayer sometimes becomes a very sterilized and generic form of religious obligation. We end up praying from our head and detach our hearts from the act. The Holy Spirit as a partner with us and the Father is a connecter of our hearts with the heart of the Father and helps us to engage prayer on a level of partnering with God in prayer instead of rattling off human requests.

Pastor Bill Johnson of Bethel Church in Redding California writes about this partnership in His book <u>Hosting the presence</u>. He puts it like this:

"Prayer is the ultimate expression of partnership with God. It is the adventure of discovering and praying His heart. So many spend their life praying to God, when they could be praying with God. This partnership, with its answers and breakthroughs, is supposed to be the source of our fullness of joy".
Bill Johnson <u>Hosting the presence</u> p.173

If we want to have powerful prayers, then we must get into the habit of allowing the Holy Spirit to come and guide them. The Holy Spirit knows the true heart of the Father, and when we pray the heart of the Father with the Holy Spirit then we stand in agreement with the will of God and experience the manifestation of His desire.

Contemplation: The act of looking at something thoughtfully for a long time; deep reflective thought.

The definition of the act of contemplation draws us to an image of oneself focusing inwardly on the presence of the Holy Spirit which dwells within us in order to gain insight and direction of prayer. This action is a time of personal reflection and engagement with the Spirit of God with the final outcome being a renewed and re inspired spirit.

"Contemplation is nothing else than a secret and peaceful and loving inflow of God, which, if not hampered, fires the soul in the spirit of love" −St. John of the Cross

"Contemplation is the light of God shining directly on the soul... The soul of the contemplative is an instrument played by the Holy Spirit" −Thomas Merton

CHAPTER

THREE

THE POWER OF INTIMACY

Intimacy is an impassioned knowledge which drives us to a heart connection with the one that we commune with. In the human sense of the word it would be like the way that I know my wife, we can almost complete each other's sentences or tell what we are each thinking at any given moment. This only happens because we spend so much time with one another intentionally wanting to know more about one another. When I know my wife's heart, I know what makes her angry, sad, happy or otherwise. In that knowledge I develop a sensitivity of how to navigate our relationship. The same goes with God, when we know His heart and what His desires and will are, then we can in a healthy way navigate our relationship and how we communicate with God in prayer.

James 1:22-25New International Version (NIV)
²² Do not merely listen to the word, and so deceive yourselves. Do what it says.²³ Anyone who listens to the word but does not do what

it says is like someone who looks at his face in a mirror [24] *and, after looking at himself, goes away and immediately forgets what he looks like.* [25] *But whoever looks intently into the perfect law that gives freedom, and continues in it—not forgetting what they have heard, but doing it—they will be blessed in what they do.*

If we want to grow in intimacy with God, then we must get to know Him in an intentional way. Spending quality time with God through the reading and **UNDERSTANDING** of His Word is the best way to get to know the heart of the Father. In the concept and practice of Lectio Divina, we are encouraged to make His Word (Lectio) our first priority. Why? Because God has laid out who He is and His desires for us in the contents of the Holy Bible.

Psalm 119:97-104 New International Version (NIV)

מ *Mem*

[97] *Oh, how I love your law!*
 I meditate on it all day long.
[98] *Your commands are always with me*
 and make me wiser than my enemies.
[99] *I have more insight than all my teachers,*
 for I meditate on your statutes.
[100] *I have more understanding than the elders,*
 for I obey your precepts.
[101] *I have kept my feet from every evil path*
 so that I might obey your word.
[102] *I have not departed from your laws,*
 for you yourself have taught me.
[103] *How sweet are your words to my taste,*
 sweeter than honey to my mouth!

[104] *I gain understanding from your precepts;*
   therefore I hate every wrong path.

The Psalmist knew that once you go from consuming the Word of God, that you must then digest its contents. The next step to intimacy is Meditatio (meditation), this is the action which allows the power of the word of God to enlighten the areas of our soul that are in conflict with the character of God. The Word of God wants to challenge the parts of our lives that are not in accordance with it so that we can lift it to God and He can deal with it. A prayer of meditation might go something like this.

"Holy and merciful father, you know all things and are known by all things. I pray right now that you search the deepest recesses of my soul and bring into alignment and correction any part of me that is in error with your true Word. As your Word is sharper than any two edged sword, would you fix your word on my heart so that it may affect any infected parts of my heart".

Psalm 130 New International Version (NIV)

Psalm 130

A song of ascents.

[1] *Out of the depths I cry to you, LORD;*
[2] *Lord, hear my voice.*
   Let your ears be attentive
   to my cry for mercy.
[3] *If you, LORD, kept a record of sins,*
   Lord, who could stand?
[4] *But with you there is forgiveness,*

so that we can, with reverence, serve you.
*⁵ I wait for the L*ORD*, my whole being waits,*
    and in his word I put my hope.
⁶ I wait for the Lord
    more than watchmen wait for the morning,
    more than watchmen wait for the morning.
*⁷ Israel, put your hope in the L*ORD*,*
    *for with the L*ORD *is unfailing love*
    and with him is full redemption.
⁸ He himself will redeem Israel
    from all their sins.

Once we have consumed and digested the Word of God, it is time to engage Him in prayer. Many times, the prayer of the Psalmist was described as a cry, it is the most expressive act of desperation which calls for a response from a wonderfully Holy and merciful God. The act of *Oratio* is prayer which calls our hearts to respond to God's Word.

Finally we let the Holy Spirit minister to us through the process which is *Contemplatio* (contemplation). This is the time when we are drawn into the loving embrace of the father which brings restoration to our soul and strengthens our intimate bond with God.

Workshop moment:

Take 20 min to spend some time reflecting on God's Word and allow Him to take you through this process to shine light on some areas of your life that need attention, to pray for His intervention, and to heal and strengthen any areas of weakness.

PRAISE HIM IN ALL THINGS

I want to make a clear point here, when I talk about praise, I am not talking about worship. I set praise apart from worship because they are two different expressions wrapped up in the same act of devotion. Worship is by definition an act of reverence paid to God, it is a ceremonial rendering of honor and homage. Praise is an expression of admiration, a way of paying tribute to, to rave about or to hail. Now praise is an act of worship but worship is very multifaceted, we worship God through our own sacrificial offerings whether it be monetary, time that we spend helping in the Church, the way that we live as living testimonies to the goodness of God, etc. When we praise God, we lift Him up with voices of adoration, we proclaim Him as the Lord of our life. Praise is what breaks the atmosphere and engages heaven on a supernatural level.

One of the things that praise does is changes the position of our hearts, when we are troubled or filled with fear over life's circumstances we have two choices; we can one just let the fear and troubles over take us and give it rule over our hearts, or we can praise God that He will bring breakthrough in the situations of life that we find ourselves. You see things in life always change, our jobs, relationships, finances, but God never changes He is the same yesterday, today, and forever. I remember early in my Christian life, I was just starting to become very aware of the reality of the enemy of my soul and my need to learn how to battle against him when I felt his presence. I was driving in my car to work one summer afternoon when I started to feel that he was harassing me. I can't recall at this time what the events where that I identified as harassment all I remember is singing praise music at the top of my lungs in the car and all of the sudden the looks that I got from the people in the car next to me. They had this look of "what is wrong with that guy"? nothing was wrong with me, but I was kicking down the gates of hell by praising the goodness of my Father in heaven.

Psalm 34New International Version (NIV)

Psalm 34

Of David. When he pretended to be insane before Abimelech, who drove him away, and he left.

[1] I will extol the LORD at all times; his praise will always be on my lips.
[2] I will glory in the LORD; let the afflicted hear and rejoice.
[3] Glorify the LORD with me; let us exalt his name together.
[4] I sought the LORD, and he answered me; he delivered me from all my fears.
[5] Those who look to him are radiant; their faces are never covered with shame.
[6] This poor man called, and the LORD heard him; he saved him out of all his troubles.
[7] The angel of the LORD encamps around those who fear him, and he delivers them.
[8] Taste and see that the LORD is good; blessed is the one who takes refuge in him.
[9] Fear the LORD, you his holy people, for those who fear him lack nothing.
[10] The lions may grow weak and hungry, but those who seek the LORD lack no good thing.
[11] Come, my children, listen to me; I will teach you the fear of the LORD.

¹² *Whoever of you loves life and desires to see many good days,*

¹³ *keep your tongue from evil and your lips from telling lies.*

¹⁴ *Turn from evil and do good; seek peace and pursue it.*

¹⁵ *The eyes of the* LORD *are on the righteous, and his ears are attentive to their cry;*

¹⁶ *but the face of the* LORD *is against those who do evil, to blot out their name from the earth.*

¹⁷ *The righteous cry out, and the* LORD *hears them; he delivers them from all their troubles.*

¹⁸ *The* LORD *is close to the brokenhearted and saves those who are crushed in spirit.*

¹⁹ *The righteous person may have many troubles, but the* LORD *delivers him from them all;*

²⁰ *he protects all his bones, not one of them will be broken.*

²¹ *Evil will slay the wicked; the foes of the righteous will be condemned.*

²² *The* LORD *will rescue his servants; no one who takes refuge in him will be condemned.*

David knew that in the midst of his troubles it was only through praise that there would be breakthrough. When we live a life of defeat, then we refuse a life of victory. We are called to be overcomers and the only way that we will be overcomers is through the power of praise in the darkest hours of life. When you read through the Psalms you see a recurring theme of David lamenting in his times of trouble and then the climate quickly turning to triumphant joy. Why? Because in his time of trial he worshipped and praised the Lord His God and praised Him also in the times of triumph.

Do we know that we as God's creations and the apple of His eye, are destined for greatness, not for troubles? Do we know that when we stop standing in agreement with the troubles of the world and start standing in agreement through our praises with God, that we will be children of breakthrough and not children of breakdown?

Let's recite this psalm over ourselves right now, and believe that in times of trial and struggle we will receive restoration through the praises of our soul standing on the promises of God.

Psalm 23New International Version (NIV)

Psalm 23

A psalm of David.

¹ *The LORD is my shepherd, I lack nothing.*
² *He makes me lie down in green pastures, he leads me beside quiet waters,*
³ *he refreshes my soul. He guides me along the right paths for his name's sake.*
⁴ *Even though I walk through the darkest valley, I will fear no evil, for you are with me;*
your rod and your staff, they comfort me.
⁵ *You prepare a table before me in the presence of my enemies; You anoint my head with oil; my cup overflows.*
⁶ *Surely your goodness and love will follow me all the days of my life, and I will dwell in the house of the LORD forever.*

I believe that praise is a response that comes from our hunger for more, it's like what we have been gorging ourselves on turns out to be unsatisfying. There are many scriptures that connect the analogy of food and spiritual hunger with what we fill our lives with. Take Isaiah 55 for example, God is calling Israel to come and drink His water, to eat His bread, to buy His food and His wine. The reason why? They have been getting their fill from the world, but God has a more fulfilling offer. When we are tired of being malnourished by the world, then our hunger for more responds in praise, seeking God for the "more" that He has to offer us.

PASSION THAT EMPOWERS

Passion: intense, driving, or overmastering feeling or conviction, a strong liking or desire for or <u>devotion</u> to some activity, object, or concept

Now these are two of the definitions of passion that I like the most, but it is not an exhaustive definition. Passion in my opinion is a force that needs to be expressed or else it will burn you up, but when you do express it the return on the emotion is a response of reciprocal love. When I speak about a passion that empowers I can only explain it from a purely human sense. If you have a husband or a wife whom you have a strong passionate love for and you do not express that passionate love, then that person's love tank will not be filled and they will not be fully capable of reciprocating a strong passion. But when we share that passion for one another, it fills that person with a passion for the other. The same thing goes for God, we all know that He loves us with an unending love, so that never changes, but when we don't passionately pursue Him then we will find that our Spirit will grow cold.

Likewise if we have a devotional life with God that is nonexistent then we will never be able to fully connect with the passionate love that He has for us. The Songs of Solomon are a beautiful tapestry of expressed passion. They are most certainly not PG-13 but they are so very empowering. When Solomon is speaking of this unbridled passion between a husband and his wife we must understand that it is symbolic of God and His bride the Church. It is a beautiful call and response between us and God, the love of the Father that we submit our hearts to be filled with elicits an equally passionate response which then is reciprocated only to keep us so continually filled with His love that we overflow that love back to His throne.

Song of Songs 2 New International Version (NIV)

Beloved

2 *I am a rose of Sharon, a lily of the valleys.*

Lover

[2] Like a lily among thorns is my darling among the young women.

Beloved

[3] Like an apple tree among the trees of the forest is my beloved among the young men.
I delight to sit in his shade, and his fruit is sweet to my taste.
[4] Let him lead me to the banquet hall, and let his banner over me be love.
[5] Strengthen me with raisins, refresh me with apples, for I am faint with love.
[6] His left arm is under my head, and his right arm embraces me.

⁷ Daughters of Jerusalem, I charge you by the gazelles and by the does of the field:

Do not arouse or awaken love until it so desires.

⁸ Listen! My beloved Look! Here he comes, leaping across the mountains, bounding over the hills.

⁹ My beloved is like a gazelle or a young stag. Look! There he stands behind our wall,

gazing through the windows, peering through the lattice.

¹⁰ My beloved spoke and said to me, "Arise, my darling, my beautiful one, come with me.

¹¹ See! The winter is past; the rains are over and gone.

¹² Flowers appear on the earth; the season of singing has come, the cooing of doves

is heard in our land.

¹³ The fig tree forms its early fruit; the blossoming vines spread their fragrance.

Arise, come, my darling; my beautiful one, come with me."

Lover

¹⁴ My dove in the clefts of the rock, in the hiding places on the mountainside,

show me your face, let me hear your voice; for your voice is sweet, and your face is lovely.

¹⁵ Catch for us the foxes, the little foxes that ruin the vineyards, our vineyards that are in bloom.

Beloved

¹⁶ My beloved is mine and I am his; he browses among the lilies.

¹⁷ Until the day breaks and the shadows flee turn, my beloved, and be like a gazelle

or like a young stag on the rugged hills.

How is your love life with Jesus? Are you pursuing Him with an unbridled passion that will fill and empower you with His response over you? Or has your passion gone cold? Often I find that I feel a coldness or a distance of relationship with the Lord, not because He has changed but because I have not been attentive to our relationship. When I have these moments in my life I make sure that I stop whatever I am doing and I go to prayer. Some of the most beautiful moments during these times is when I hear the Lord say to me "I love you, I always loved you, I will always love you" it's so definitive and absolute, there is no question in the mind of Christ of how He loves us and desires us. He is a passionate and loving God who wants to pour out His love on us without limit.

When I think about those who have gone before us in the faith who were filled with a Holy zeal, an unquenchable passion for more of the Lord, I think about the apostles. The men and women who dedicated themselves to seeking deeper intimacy and relationship with the Lord on a daily basis. These are people who have had a tangible encounter with the presence of the living God and decided that it was worth engaging in a deeper way. The Disciples of Christ pressed in daily to seek Him more, Moses entered into the tent on a regular basis to engage the presence of God in an intimate way, and his sidekick Joshua was so captivated by what came from Moses' tent that he just wanted to rest in the presence that dwelt there. That is a passion that empowers, all of these people who passionately pursued the presence of God received something supernatural. Moses received guidance, direction, favor, the disciples received the baptism of the Holy Spirit which unlocked heavenly gifts and the miraculous.

When we pursue Christ with and abandoned passion that has no limits, we will experience an outpouring that is filled with the great power of His presence. It isn't about what we receive in the gifts, the empowering gift is the reciprocated passion that God pursues us with.

LIVING A SATURATED LIFE

According to Jewish culture, something isn't considered full unless it is overflowing. Imagine a washcloth, when a washcloth is dry and used up, the fibers are brittle and when you twist or stretch that cloth it is susceptible to tearing apart. When the same cloth is completely saturated, when you go to twist or stretch it then the liquid that has saturated that cloth will spill out.

As Christians many of us are dry washcloths, we have given and given and given but because we have not returned to the well to be saturated again we have become dry, and under stress we fall apart.

When I think of saturated lives I think of the disciples after the day of Pentecost.

Acts 3:1-10New International Version (NIV)

Peter Heals a Lame Beggar

3 One day Peter and John were going up to the temple at the time of prayer—at three in the afternoon. ² Now a man who was lame from birth was being carried to the temple gate called Beautiful, where he was put every day to beg from those going into the temple courts. ³ When he saw Peter and John about to enter, he asked them for money. ⁴ Peter looked straight at him, as did John. Then Peter said, "Look at us!" ⁵ So the man gave them his attention, expecting to get something from them.

⁶ Then Peter said, "Silver or gold I do not have, but what I do have I give you. In the name of Jesus Christ of Nazareth, walk." ⁷ Taking him by the right hand, he helped him up, and instantly the man's feet and ankles became strong. ⁸ He jumped to his feet and began to walk. Then he went with them into the temple courts, walking and jumping, and praising God. ⁹ When all the people saw him walking and praising God, ¹⁰ they recognized him as the same man who used to sit begging at the temple gate called Beautiful, and they were filled with wonder and amazement at what had happened to him.

Acts 4:12-16New International Version (NIV)
¹² Salvation is found in no one else, for there is no other name under heaven given to mankind by which we must be saved."

¹³ When they saw the courage of Peter and John and realized that they were unschooled, ordinary men, they were astonished and they took note that these men had been with Jesus. ¹⁴ But since they could see the man who had been healed standing there with them, there was nothing they could say. ¹⁵ So they ordered them to withdraw from the Sanhedrin and then conferred together.¹⁶ "What are we going to do with these men?" they asked. "Everyone living in Jerusalem knows they have performed a notable sign, and we cannot deny it.

The apostles of the Lord where saturated, so much so that when they were squeezed they overflowed the presence of God. When we read these two accounts and we go back a chapter or two, we see that they spent time praising God and fellowshipping together. Whenever they went out and engaged the people, they would go back and get saturated in the presence of God. If we are wanting to be people who live and operate in the presence of God, we must make sure that we constantly fill ourselves with Him. Even Jesus when He was exhausted from all of the ministry that He was doing would take the time to get alone with the Father so that He could be recharged and prepared to go back out into the field.

Our Passionate pursuit of God goes hand in hand with our being saturated by His presence. In 1 Thessalonians 5:19 we are cautioned to not quench the Holy Spirit, the word quench is translated in the original language as to extinguish. This action would describe a passion that has gone cold. We must fan our passion for Jesus into flame through our relentless pursuit of relationship with the lover of our soul.

Moses, one of the patriarchs of the faith practiced this saturating relationship with God on a regular basis. One of the times when Moses went to get soaked by the presence of God was in Exodus 33.

Exodus 33:7-11 New International Version (NIV)

The Tent of Meeting

⁷ Now Moses used to take a tent and pitch it outside the camp some distance away, calling it the "tent of meeting." Anyone inquiring of the LORD would go to the tent of meeting outside the camp. ⁸ And whenever Moses went out to the tent, all the people rose and stood at the entrances to their tents, watching Moses until he entered the tent. ⁹ As Moses went into the tent, the pillar of cloud would come down and stay at the entrance, while the LORD spoke with Moses. ¹⁰ Whenever the people saw the pillar of cloud standing at the entrance to the tent, they all stood and worshiped, each at the entrance to their tent.¹¹ The LORD would speak to Moses face to face, as one speaks to a friend. Then Moses would return to the camp, but his young aide Joshua son of Nun did not leave the tent.

In these verses we see what Moses' action was, he would go into his secret place and seek the presence of the Lord. It was in the previous chapter that Moses came down from his pilgrimage up Mt. Sinai and saw that the Israelites had in their impatience fashioned an idol to worship. Moses was in a place where he was under distress and new that he needed to seek the Lord for refreshing and refilling while trying to lead these people. After his time with the Lord we receive God's response.

Exodus 33:12-19 New International Version (NIV)

Moses and the Glory of the LORD

¹² *Moses said to the LORD, "You have been telling me, 'Lead these people,' but you have not let me know whom you will send with me. You have said, 'I know you by name and you have found favor with me.' ¹³ If you are pleased with me, teach me your ways so I may know you and continue to find favor with you. Remember that this nation is your people."*

¹⁴ *The LORD replied, "My Presence will go with you, and I will give you rest."*

15 Then Moses said to him, "If your Presence does not go with us, do not send us up from here. 16 How will anyone know that you are pleased with me and with your people unless you go with us? What else will distinguish me and your people from all the other people on the face of the earth?"

17 And the LORD said to Moses, "I will do the very thing you have asked, because I am pleased with you and I know you by name."

18 Then Moses said, "Now show me your glory."

19 And the LORD said, "I will cause all my goodness to pass in front of you, and I will proclaim my name, the LORD, in your presence.

The response was that Moses would be covered with the Glory of God Almighty. The saturation that we receive from God when we go before Him and soak in His presence is a saturation of His glory. When we read this passage of scripture we can see that it is only when we are saturated with this glory that the Lord is recognizable in our lives and ministries. Dry people who attempt to operate in dryness do not reflect the presence of God upon them, but people who are constantly in the presence of God to receive a fresh anointing and impartation carry the presence of God with them and it is visible to everyone who they come across.

Workshop moment: Let's pray for a fresh anointing a fresh impartation of the Glory of God to saturate your soul.

Lord, I ask for a waterfall of your glory to saturate my soul. Would you show yourself strong to me as I present myself before you.

CHAPTER

FOUR

WHAT IS SPIRITUAL ATTACK?

Let me open this session by first letting you know that many people in the Church and even outside of the Church are under tremendous Spiritual attack and they don't even know it. Because Spiritual attack embeds itself in our circumstances it's very easy to dismiss what you may be experiencing as a side effect of your current condition. Now sometimes that may be true, but what we need to be observant about is the duration and impact that these episodes have on our lives.

According to Ryan LeStrange, author of <u>Overcoming spiritual attack</u> the definition of spiritual attack is as follows:

"A spiritual attack is a series of events coordinated by the demonic realms to oppress the believer, abort promises, shipwreck faith, and stall out destiny". P 9 Overcoming spiritual attack

That seems like a fairly clear cut understanding of what Spiritual attack is, but then he elaborates on the definition by informing us that the way the enemy launches a spiritual attack on the believer is by launching accusations, plans, persecutions, and circumstances in an attempt to disconnect the believer from their destiny and identity in the kingdom of God. One instance in scripture that we find which validates this definition is right in the beginning of the Bible.

Genesis 3 New International Version (NIV)

The Fall

3 *Now the serpent was more crafty than any of the wild animals the LORD God had made. He said to the woman, "Did God really say, 'You must not eat from any tree in the garden'?"*

² The woman said to the serpent, "We may eat fruit from the trees in the garden, ³ but God did say, 'You must not eat fruit from the tree that is in the middle of the garden, and you must not touch it, or you will die.'"

⁴ "You will not certainly die," the serpent said to the woman. ⁵ "For God knows that when you eat from it your eyes will be opened, and you will be like God, knowing good and evil."

In this account with Adam and Eve in the garden we see the following:

1. They are in the garden, the place where the presence and glory of God dwells. The garden was created to be an eternal dwelling place for the creation. I would liken the garden to our future eternal dwelling place in the Kingdom of God.

2. The deceiver came in a very "covert" or "undercover" manner, he is described as being very sneaky and deceptive.
3. Satan questions the authority of God and attempts to deceive Eve into doing the same.
4. He creates in inner conflict which causes us to be divided in our heart from God.

It's funny because what the enemy does is he tries to gain our trust and put us at ease by giving us a false assurance. The line that sticks out to me in this segment of scripture is when satan says *"you will not certainly die"* ….. yeah sure not right away at least but what we know from scripture is that Adam and Eve were created to be immortal, they were not created for death but when they fell for the scheme of the enemy death became a part of their reality. Think about some of the ways the enemy might be trying to draw you into a deception that would lead to death. What vices have you fallen to that are not in God's will for your life? Drug use? Alcohol abuse? Pornography? Pride? Selfish ambition? Yeah maybe none of these things will kill us right away although some might, but what happens is when we engage in something that is outside of the will of God for our life and you physically survive, then we are deceiving yourself by thinking that there are no negative consequences.

For Adam and Eve their consequence was contention with God, with one another, and the destruction of their original created purpose. Spiritual attack gets us to deny and defy God, creates a contentious relationship with one another, and distorts our identity and our destiny.

HOW TO IDENTIFY SPIRITUAL ATTACK

Who are we? We are children of the living God, created to be in relationship with Him, and since we are created to be in relationship we must know Him and be able to discern His voice and character.

John 10:1-6 New International Version (NIV)

The Good Shepherd and His Sheep

10 *"Very truly I tell you Pharisees, anyone who does not enter the sheep pen by the gate, but climbs in by some other way, is a thief and a robber. ² The one who enters by the gate is the shepherd of the sheep.³ The gatekeeper opens the gate for him, and the sheep listen to his voice. He calls his own sheep by name and leads them out. ⁴ When he has brought out all his own, he goes on ahead of them, and his sheep follow him because they know his voice. ⁵ But they will never follow a stranger; in fact, they will run away from him because they do not recognize a stranger's voice." ⁶ Jesus used this figure of speech, but the Pharisees did not understand what he was telling them.*

The parable of the shepherd and His flock gives us a good picture of how we can identify spiritual attack and how things can go wrong if we are not discerning the voice of God. In the soul of the believer the Holy Spirit is your gatekeeper, He is the one that you have been sealed with as a mark of salvation. The voice of God is recognizable by the one who has learned how to develop a sensitivity with the Holy Spirit to identify the voice of God. It is like a divine security system that recognizes intruders and immediately locks the doors to not allow any unwanted guests. The issue is that we also have the ability to activate this system or shut it off, when we don't activate the system then we open ourselves up to be deceived by the voice of the enemy because we have no way of verifying the voice.

Do you know how to discern the voice of God? His voice brings peace, it edifies, exhorts, lines up with scripture, and brings glory to Jesus. So we can easily assume that the voice of the enemy brings anxiety, defeats confidence, destroys identity, opposes scripture, and glorifies self.

John 8:44 New International Version (NIV)

[44] *You belong to your father, the devil, and you want to carry out your father's desires. He was a murderer from the beginning, not holding to the truth, for there is no truth in him. When he lies, he speaks his native language, for he is a liar and the father of lies.*

So first and foremost, in order for someone to properly identify if what they are experiencing is a spiritual attack, they must know the voice of God. Second we need to understand our enemy and know the methods of attack that he uses to try and defeat us.

1.   The enemy works to discourage us:

When we engage our faith, our God given purpose and destiny, we will come against certain opposition. One of the ways the enemy does this is by bringing discouragement by using present insecurities that we may have within ourselves. The voice of the enemy tells us "we aren't good enough, educated enough, and competent enough" etc. the enemy will often times try to make us feel insecure about what God wants to do through us. He tells us that no one cares about what we have to say, or that we are going to look foolish. His ultimate goal is to extinguish our zeal for what we sense the Lord doing in us. The voice of the enemy attempts to disqualify you from your calling, the fleshly response to this level of opposition is to give up and just go about business as usual. But if we know the voice and character of God, He is raising you up not to fit in or measure up to the qualifications of man but to be a trailblazer, to be set apart for a mission that is unique to you and God. Paul spoke of this being set apart when he wrote Romans, he proclaimed himself to be set apart for the purpose of being a servant of God and now reserves the right to be called an apostle.

I believe that the reason why this is such an effective tactic of the enemy is that it works in our insecurities and plays on our broken identity in Christ. When we exalt leaders and make their accomplishments something that we ourselves pursue then we will ultimately be defeated by discouragement. But if we as Paul says in Ephesians to be imitators of Christ and not of men, then our courage will not be shaken but fortified in Christ.

2. He wants to sterilize your faith:

    I sadly see this very often and myself was nearly a victim of this sneak attack. It's found in the zeal of the new believer who goes from zero to one hundred miles per hour in their faith life. They devour everything that they can from Bible studies and small groups, they are involved in every kind of ministry opportunity that comes their way, but they miss a key element…their own soul state. They became too consumed with doing that they stopped being, they have ceased getting into the presence of God and allowing Him to minister to them when their heart and soul is groaning.

I have seen it in the seminary student who has been called, set apart, anointed for ministry, but what they have neglected is allowing the spirit of God to pour back into them what they have poured out. It is a stagnant if not dead prayer life which leads to burnout and often times forfeiting of calling.

So how does the enemy work in this situation? He is the encourager of your avoidance of engaging with your heavenly Father. He is their cheering you on when you are pursuing your calling or your faith all in your own strength. The victory for the enemy is getting us to ignore or disconnect from God, it renders us passionless for the presence and keeps us on a spiritual life support through meaningless servitude. We see it every Sunday morning in Churches all across the country, it is Sunday morning attendance, Sunday morning serving, but there is no joy, no excitement, no zeal for the Lord or His presence. The reason why the enemy attacks our faith is because then it renders us disconnected from the power source that brings the presence of God into the ministry that we have been called to. It closes the door to the miraculous, it shuts down the gifts, it renders the believer spiritually sterile. I would liken it to a car, you turn the car on, it's all gassed up, the engine is running, the battery is strong, but if it's in neutral it's simply motionless.

Along with this method of spiritual attack, the enemy makes an attempt to get you to question your calling. Many times this attack comes when we are pressing in for breakthrough but grow tired during the process. It's the Pastor or layman in the church who has been toiling for breakthrough but has only been met with more toiling. It's the mom or dad who have been praying for God's intervention in a marriage or for their children and they have only experienced more heartbreak and have become tired of contending. When these things happen often times it's sad to say the result is a Pastor leaving ministry, a layman leaving their Church, or a mom or dad leaving a marriage. You know Jesus came under the same attack that we often times come under.

John 4:1-11 New International Version

Jesus Is Tested in the Wilderness

4 *Then Jesus was led by the Spirit into the wilderness to be tempted by the devil.* ² *After fasting forty days and forty nights, he was hungry.³ The tempter came to him and said, "If you are the Son of God, tell these stones to become bread."*

⁴ *Jesus answered, "It is written: 'Man shall not live on bread alone, but on every word that comes from the mouth of God.'"*

⁵ *Then the devil took him to the holy city and had him stand on the highest point of the temple.* ⁶ *"If you are the Son of God," he said, "throw yourself down. For it is written:*

"'He will command his angels concerning you, and they will lift you up in their hands, so that you will not strike your foot against a stone.'"

7 Jesus answered him, "It is also written: 'Do not put the Lord your God to the test.'"

8 Again, the devil took him to a very high mountain and showed him all the kingdoms of the world and their splendor. 9 "All this I will give you," he said, "if you will bow down and worship me."

10 Jesus said to him, "Away from me, Satan! For it is written: 'Worship the Lord your God, and serve him only."

11 Then the devil left him, and angels came and attended him.

The enemy attempted to get Jesus to forfeit His calling while He was in His final hours of contending in the wilderness. Again it's when we find ourselves in the final hours of our contending, when breakthrough is on the horizon that the attack comes in an attempt to get us to forfeit what we have been called to.

3. He attacks your emotions:

    Now I want to make something very clear, I am not talking about diagnosed emotional disorders like depression, what I want to talk about is how the enemy during the course of attack can make us feel depressed, or anxious, or confused.

Often times when we are engaging in the faith, when we are seeking a deeper relationship with Christ and all that comes with it, that we come under an attack that causes us to feel unusual emotions. The typical response when we feel this overwhelming onslaught of emotion is to withdraw. If the enemy can get you to remove yourself from the community or the people who can truly help you through your attack, then he is winning the battle for your destiny.

One such account in scripture where this level of spiritual attack was waged against someone was in 1 kings 19 when the life of Elijah came under attack from Jezebel. In the preceding chapter Elijah in his boldness challenged the prophets of Baal and Asherah that if they were truly Gods to call on them to manifest miracles and signs. But no matter how hard they prayed and sacrificed to the Gods, nothing happened. Yahweh was proven to be the only true God and the prophets of Baal and Asherah were put to death. In chapter 19 we read that Jezebel was irate with the actions of Elijah and threatened to take his life. Elijah became distressed it said and wished for God to take his life.

1 Kings 19:1-5 New International Version (NIV)

Elijah Flees to Horeb

19 *Now Ahab told Jezebel everything Elijah had done and how he had killed all the prophets with the sword.* *² So Jezebel sent a messenger to Elijah to say, "May the gods deal with me, be it ever so severely, if by this time tomorrow I do not make your life like that of one of them."*

³ Elijah was afraid and ran for his life. When he came to Beersheba in Judah, he left his servant there, *⁴ while he himself went a day's journey into the wilderness. He came to a broom bush, sat down under it and prayed that he might die. "I have had enough, LORD,"* *he said. "Take my life; I am no better than my ancestors." ⁵ Then he lay down under the bush and fell asleep.*

So what do we find from this exchange? When we fight against the enemy we can be sure that he will launch a counter attack. Elijah became so distressed at the attack of the enemy that he wished for God to take his life and he withdrew to Horeb. It is very common for people to run when they feel pressure from the enemy coming against them Horeb is translated as meaning desert or destruction, when we decide to run to a place where we think we will find shelter often times we run to a desert that will lead to our destruction. We cry out to God presenting Him with our loyalty and faithfulness to Him almost imploring Him to end the advancement of the enemy, but at the end of the day attack is going to happen when we fight the kingdom of darkness, and when the attack comes we must resolve to stand firm in the faith with an unwavering authority in Jesus Christ.

Ultimately the attack on our emotions starts in the mind, in Elijah's situation he allowed his mind to become consumed with the thought that Jezebel was going to kill him out of retaliation for destroying the prophets of Baal. Just like Elijah, the enemy wants to attack our minds by flooding us with thoughts that are completely untrue. He likes to attack your insecurities and he attempts to flood your mind with discouraging thoughts which directly affect your calling and your identity in Christ.

4. He wants you to throw in the towel:

"Just give up! I know it's hard trying to do everything perfect to try to please God, so just give up, no one would blame you, if anything you should be rewarded for trying so hard". This is something like what a monologue from hell sounds like, satan attempts to validate a feeling of defeat and give you a sense of justification for giving it all up. It is at this point when we become the most vulnerable to give up the fight and regress back into our old ways. The loss of Hope is the open window to a defeated heart. When we give up hope in something that the Lord has called us to do whether it be because we aren't contending enough, or we aren't patient enough, then we open our hearts up to defeat. But something creeps in before defeat…depression. When hope is lost then we enter into a depressed state as though everything is lost. We give up on the dreams that we once had and we start to question our abilities and our calling. When this happens more often than not we forfeit the fight.

Luke 24:13-24 New International Version (NIV)

On the Road to Emmaus

¹³ Now that same day two of them were going to a village called Emmaus, about seven mile from Jerusalem. ¹⁴ They were talking with each other about everything that had happened. ¹⁵ As they talked and discussed these things with each other, Jesus himself came up and walked along with them; ¹⁶ but they were kept from recognizing him.

¹⁷ He asked them, "What are you discussing together as you walk along?"

They stood still, their faces downcast. ¹⁸ One of them, named Cleopas, asked him, "Are you the only one visiting Jerusalem who does not know the things that have happened there in these days?"

19 "What things?" he asked.

"About Jesus of Nazareth," they replied. "He was a prophet, powerful in word and deed before God and all the people. 20 The chief priests and our rulers handed him over to be sentenced to death, and they crucified him; 21 but we had hoped that he was the one who was going to redeem Israel. And what is more, it is the third day since all this took place. 22 In addition, some of our women amazed us. They went to the tomb early this morning 23 but didn't find his body. They came and told us that they had seen a vision of angels, who said he was alive. 24 Then some of our companions went to the tomb and found it just as the women had said, but they did not see Jesus."

Let us focus on the section of this passage when Cleopas and his companion seemingly defaulted to categorize Christ as a prophet and nothing more. They claimed that Jesus did good things but did not fulfill their hopes as the savior they were praying for. Their focus was on the perception of defeat at the hands of the cross, they saw the death of a physical body and the absence of a resurrected Christ as sign that He was not the real thing.

When we labor and toil in the name of the Lord with no immediate result it is so easy to fall to the deception of the enemy that says "see! Nothing, you did it all for nothing just give up" whether your labor produces a physical result or not doesn't mean that God is or isn't doing something through your efforts it just means that God shows up however He desires in the moment. Notice how Jesus came along the travels of these two downtrodden men, it says that they didn't recognize Him. Sometimes Jesus works in ways that we may not recognize, so no need to throw in the towel when things transpire in ways that look foreign to us, it just shows us that God is at work.

WHAT IS THE DIFFERENCE BETWEEN OPPRESSION AND POSSESSION?

Why do we have to understand what oppression and possession are when we are learning about spiritual warfare? The answer is simple, when we are learning the ways that the enemy operates when attempting to derail the believer from their identity, purpose, and relationship with God, we must also understand what I believe are the extreme categories and side effects of spiritual attack that has gone untreated. In my opinion and what I have observed from doing healing ministry, the way that the enemy operates is as follows.

Spiritual attack, which is any attack on the believer to deceive them mentally, attacking them emotionally, and robbing them spiritually.

Oppression, is the side effect of an agreement that the believer makes with the lie that the enemy has spoken over them either directly or indirectly. It gives an authority for the enemy to "hitchhike" in a sense on the mind of the believer, corrupting their thoughts about themselves and others, and altering their attention from God to their condition.

Possession, is when the person has given themselves completely over to a foreign enemy to operate through them. This oftentimes happens through occult practices, un Biblical observances, un Godly oaths and soul ties to the demonic.

So now that we understand the differences between oppression and possession I want to make something clear.

In my theological understanding and in my observance of what I have experienced in ministry, a person who has the Holy Spirit in them cannot be possessed. You are a single occupancy dwelling, you can either allow the Holy Spirit to occupy, or you can allow the enemy to occupy, but you cannot have two roommates.

John 8:36 New International Version (NIV)
36 So if the Son sets you free, you will be free indeed.

John 8:36 is not a conditional statement, it is definitive. If you give yourself to Christ and invite the Holy Spirit to dwell within you, you cannot also give room for the devil to dwell. Now someone who is under oppression is just experiencing the side effects of a spiritual attack that they have given agreement to. When we come under spiritual attack we understand from the previous session that the enemy comes in to distort our identity and destiny by creating dissention between us and God. When the enemy plants lies into your mind and your heart about you, God, you're calling, your destiny etc. and we give into the lies then we live in a state of spiritual oppression.

Spiritual oppression isn't just a "bad day" it's an ongoing onslaught of the enemy that he uses to disrupt your world. Oppression is a continual action that will occur until the oppressed comes to the realization of what is going on and make the effort to be set free. I would like to say that I don't know anyone who decides that they want to live under enemy oppression, but then I would be lying. I know that there are people who become so used to living as oppressed beings, that they don't know what they would do with themselves if they weren't. These people love the sympathy of others, they love when people feel bad for them and they reflect a victimized Spirit. These people more often than not will attach themselves to people who are free for the sake of leeching them of their peace.

WHY DOES THE ENEMY ATTACK US?

There are a myriad of reasons why the enemy launches his relentless attacks on us, and it all starts at our destiny.

*Jeremiah 29:11*New International Version (NIV)
¹¹ For I know the plans I have for you," declares the LORD, "plans to prosper you and not to harm you, plans to give you hope and a future.

This is reason one why the enemy attacks, from the point of our coming into the world (where the enemy has dominion) we have a target on our backs. It's the future promise that God has for our lives that the enemy never wants us to grab a hold of, the reason is that this future promise and destiny is a direct threat to the kingdom of darkness.

The second reason why the enemy launches an attack on a believer is when they are on the verge of breakthrough. Let me clarify what I mean by breakthrough, breakthrough is a moment of personal and kingdom advancement. It is when a person who doesn't believe in Christ is on the verge of making a confession of faith, it's when the new believer is stepping into a deeper relationship with Jesus, it's when the mature believer who has been contending for a person or a ministry is on the verge of their prayers being fulfilled.

Luke 22 New International Version (NIV)

Judas Agrees to Betray Jesus

22 *Now the Festival of Unleavened Bread, called the Passover, was approaching,* **²** *and the chief priests and the teachers of the law were looking for some way to get rid of Jesus, for they were afraid of the people.* **³** *Then Satan entered Judas, called Iscariot, one of the Twelve.* **⁴** *And Judas went to the chief priests and the officers of the temple guard and discussed with them how he might betray Jesus.* **⁵** *They were delighted and agreed to give him money.* **⁶** *He consented, and watched for an opportunity to hand Jesus over to them when no crowd was present.*

Look at the Judas scenario, it says that as Passover was approaching. What is so significant about Passover? This would be the very last event that Jesus would organize before His going to the cross. In the tradition of the *Pesach* or Passover, people would rid their homes of any food item that contained leaven as a symbol of purification. Certainly the disciples followed the same order for Passover as seen in Luke 22:7-13. Now although we understand that there is a cultural piece to this physical cleansing, we must understand that there is also a symbolic spiritual cleansing that takes place as well.

I believe that Judas failed to spiritually cleanse himself, it says that Satan **entered** him. What was Satan doing in their? I think he was searching for a heart issue that he could manipulate so that he could keep Judas from receiving what Christ would have to offer him through His sacrifice. What we come to find out after this betrayal Judas was filled with so much guilt that he took his own life.

The disciples that moved forward with Jesus came to experience one of the most defining moments in their walk on the day of Pentecost. It was here that they were filled with the power of the Holy Spirit, the promised one of Jesus who baptized them with fire to fulfill the mandate of the miraculous, but Judas was not among them.

When we engage the deeper levels of our relationship with Christ we need to be fully aware that the enemy of our soul will attempt to attack us at our weakest point. For some it may be love of money, popularity, unfulfilled emotional needs, insecurities etc. he will do whatever it takes to attack those points in an attempt to get you to chase the desire of your flesh that has not been submitted to Jesus so that you will pursue your flesh and not the lover of your soul. Let's take a look at another person who was compromised by the enemy and shipwrecked his destiny.

*1 Samuel 13:9-12*New International Version (NIV)
⁹ So he said, "Bring me the burnt offering and the fellowship offerings." And Saul offered up the burnt offering. ¹⁰ Just as he finished making the offering, Samuel arrived, and Saul went out to greet him.

¹¹ "What have you done?" asked Samuel.

Saul replied, "When I saw that the men were scattering, and that you did not come at the set time, and that the Philistines were assembling at Mikmash, ¹² I thought, 'Now the Philistines will come down against me at Gilgal, and I have not sought the LORD's favor.' So I felt compelled to offer the burnt offering."

Saul was afraid, in the preceding verses Saul was commanded by Samuel to wait seven days before making advancements against the Philistine army. The reason for this was that God was going to prepare an opportunity for Saul and his fear filled army to overtake their enemy. But Saul in his pride and fear defied the orders of God through the Prophet Samuel and made a burnt offering in an attempt to appease God. This was an example of outright defiance and willful sin, Saul knew what he should have done but says that he felt "compelled". Samuel goes on to rebuke Saul for the foolish thing that he did and warns him that now he will fall out of favor with God and he will be replaced by a man who is after the very heart of God.

Victory was at hand for Saul as long as he continued to listen to the Lord and didn't fall into the trap of self-fulfillment. We always desire what is in our best interests, but do we ever think about what God's best interests are for us? This is what the enemy goes after, he tries to get us to a place where we reject the "waiting on God" period and go after what we ultimately want to do anyway.

So how can we apply these experiences to what we may potentially experience as believers in Christ?

1. It's the new believer who experiences a tragedy in their life. When their faith isn't strong enough to endure the heartache of the loss of a loved one. The enemy wants to find that entrance to their most vulnerable place and implant the lie that causes the person to question the goodness of God.
2. It's the hungry believer who has a desire to seek the deeper things of God but with little result. The enemy comes in with the lie that tells them that the reason why they don't witness the miraculous

is because they don't have enough faith, or that the gifts are dead.

3. It's the seasoned believer who has been contending for breakthrough in their life or the lives of others but is growing tired. The enemy plants the lie that there will be no breakthrough and their efforts are useless.

What do all of these people have in common? Breakthrough, on a personal and a corporate level. Breakthrough was sure to come but the enemy hijacked it through doubt and defeat. We grow stronger in faith and our relationship with Jesus through adversity and trials. What does Paul say?

Romans 5:3-5 New International Version (NIV)
³ Not only so, but we also glory in our sufferings, because we know that suffering produces perseverance; ⁴ perseverance, character; and character, hope. ⁵ And hope does not put us to shame, because God's love has been poured out into our hearts through the Holy Spirit, who has been given to us.

CHAPTER

FIVE

IMPACT ON THE MIND AND BODY

Just like spiritual attack can take a toll on one's emotions by instilling fear, frustration, anger, and other emotions, it can also be manifested in your mind and body. Spiritual attack can lead us to have irrational or unreasonable thoughts (paranoia) and can even create mental confusion and alter our mental perception about certain events or occurrences i.e. misinterpreting conversations or creating a false scenario or outcome of certain events.

*Matthew 17:14-18*New International Version (NIV)
Jesus Heals a Demon-Possessed Boy
14 When they came to the crowd, a man approached Jesus and knelt before him. 15 "Lord, have mercy on my son," he said. "He has seizures and is suffering greatly. He often falls into the fire or into the water. 16 I brought him to your disciples, but they could not heal him."

This is an account where the enemy clearly afflicted his subject in more than one way, but what we see the primary affliction was mental. The word that the author uses to describe the boys affliction is the Greek word *seleniazomai* which is translated as moonstruck or crazy. I don't know what the indirect cause of this boy's suffering was, but the lunar cycle is culprit in the term moonstruck. Now whether the mental affliction had to do with an occultic following or worship or not is unknown, but what we do know is that the point of affliction caused the boy's mental instability and therefore influenced him to attempt to kill himself. In this account I ponder if suicide is a side effect of a spiritually oppressed mind. If the enemy seeks to steal, kill, and destroy, then why would that not be a possibility?

A few of the ways that I would attempt to identify if you are displaying symptom of spiritual attack on your mind are as follows:

1. Do you process conversations that you have with others as directly negative towards you personally? The enemy wants you to misinterpret what others are saying and oftentimes gets you to believe that what they said is an attack on you.

2. Do you feel like people are talking about you? Or that they are conspiring against you? Paranoia of things that aren't actually happening is a tool that the enemy uses to get your mind focused on a mirage of things and off of what God is wanting to do.

3. Thoughts of dying? Or taking your life? The enemy wants to make you think that your life has no value. He might attempt to do this by making you believe that you are unloved, unlikable, useless, a failure etc. he wants to destroy you so that you can no longer be

used for the glory of God and the advancement of His kingdom, and if he can get you to buy into these lies and get you to a place where he can convince you to take your life then he wins.

4. Distorted or demonic dreams: Many times when one is experiencing certain types of emotional or spiritual stress, they create an open door for the enemy to attack your dreams. For example…if someone is experiencing a stress in their marriage, the enemy might send a spirit to seduce them in their dreams. This spirit will fulfill the unfulfilled desires of the person. In these instances we need to ask ourselves… what was the feeling in the dream? What was your emotional response to the dream or in the dream? If none of your answers line up with an emption or a feeling that reflects the character of God, then you just got attacked.

I wonder if the susceptibility of our minds being attacked is the very reason why we are admonished by the Apostle Paul to make sure that our minds are in a posture that prepares itself to receive only what is of God and none of what is from the enemy.

Colossians 3 New International Version (NIV)
Living as Those Made Alive in Christ

3 *Since, then, you have been raised with Christ, set your hearts on things above, where Christ is, seated at the right hand of God.* *²Set your minds on things above, not on earthly things.* *³For you died, and your life is now hidden with Christ in God.* *⁴When Christ, who is your life, appears, then you also will appear with him in glory.*

So how about you? Have you been having irrational thoughts that people have been talking about you? Have you had feelings of death or feelings like your life is worthless? How about hearing things in a conversation that weren't really said? Then you may have or may be experiencing spiritual attack on your mind.

So how about the physical? Can a spiritual attack show physical signs? Yes! Now again I will leave you with this disclaimer that sometimes when someone is sick they are simply just that...sick, but there are times when I believe the sickness is a sign of a spiritual oppression.

Luke 13:11-16 New International Version (NIV)
[11] and a woman was there who had been crippled by a spirit for eighteen years. She was bent over and could not straighten up at all. [12] When Jesus saw her, he called her forward and said to her, "Woman, you are set free from your infirmity." [13] Then he put his hands on her, and immediately she straightened up and praised God.

[14] Indignant because Jesus had healed on the Sabbath, the synagogue leader said to the people, "There are six days for work. So come and be healed on those days, not on the Sabbath."

[15] The Lord answered him, "You hypocrites! Doesn't each of you on the Sabbath untie your ox or donkey from the stall and lead it out to give it water? [16] Then should not this woman, a daughter of Abraham, whom Satan has kept bound for eighteen long years, be set free on the Sabbath day from what bound her?"

It is clear that this was most likely a woman who was a follower of Yahweh, as she is described as a "daughter of Abraham". Now what we don't necessarily know is why this woman afflicted by Satan. Well the heading of this chapter is titled "repent or perish", the heading of the chapter may lead us to wonder if unrepented sin leading to an open door for the enemy to enter could result in a physical infirmity at the hands of Satan.

A few years ago when I was involved with a local Church's healing and deliverance ministry I had a man come to me and my partner for a prayer session. Now originally he came to ask for healing from a frozen shoulder. This condition medically takes a lot of treatment from medicinal to physical therapy and takes a lot of time to clear up. As my partner and I entered into prayer we started to hear many layers of unresolved issues that were rooted in unforgiveness and broken family relationship. Well an hour of prayer came and went and not once did we actually pray over his shoulder, but the next day after he had reconciled his strained family relationship his shoulder was healed. This was a case where the symptom of inner brokenness showed up as a physical illness. Many doctors will tell you that lots of times people that have heavy levels of stress make themselves physically sick, well can't that be the same for people who are spiritually oppressed?

So how can we discern whether or not what you may be experiencing in the physical is a result of a Spiritual condition or is simply just physical?

1. Pray: there is no substitute for going directly to God to help give insight into your current condition.
2. Enter into sincere repentance: This is a point where there needs to be brutal honesty and transparency. If you have any current or former issues that have not been properly dealt with, then you still have an

open door for the enemy to afflict you. Some of these may be:

- Un-forgiveness
- Ungodly worship (Occult, witchcraft, Ouija, etc.)
- Sexual sin (pornography, homosexuality, etc.)
- Drug or alcohol addiction
- Violent or abusive tendencies

3. Do you have abnormally low levels of energy, especially when it comes to doing ministry? Often times a spiritual attack on the body manifests in abnormal fatigue when attempting to engage in ministry in some capacity. You tend to just feel lethargy when you even think about ministry.

4. Talk to your Pastor: If you have a Pastor who has been trained in inner healing and deliverance set up a time to do some searching with a couple of trained leaders to help you sift through some tough places so that you may gain freedom.

IMPACT ON YOUR CALLING AND DESTINY

I believe that there are two ways in which the enemy attacks or sideswipes your calling, first he will attempt to rob you of your passion for the mission that God has called you to. Just like I expressed in the previous chapter how the enemy attempts to sterilize the faith of a believer by robbing them of their zeal, he does the same thing for the man or woman who is already in ministry.

Ministry is an emotionally and spiritually draining endeavor and Satan knows that when you have been laboring you become susceptible. As a Church planter I can tell you what the element of attack looks like, it attacks your confidence in yourself and in God and gets you to question calling. Pastoring a Church or ministry in general is a marathon not a sprint, but for so many leaders in the Church they become weary of not seeing expected results and they start to doubt calling and doubt God's involvement in their ministry. The same goes for the person who is in lay leadership. Maybe your small group or your volunteer ministry isn't growing the way that you expected it to, or maybe you feel like you have been putting in a lot of effort and seeing no results. This is where the enemy wants to attack your calling by instilling doubt. I can imagine that this is how Moses felt when he verbally disqualified himself as one who could be used by God to influence a nation. You see Moses was chosen by God to be the vessel that was used to influence Pharaoh to release the Jews from Egyptian captivity and lead them on their journey to a new land. But Moses experienced push back and reluctance from the people on multiple occasions and grew discouraged. He blamed his poor speech, and questioned God's plan. He asks God in Exodus 6:12 why would Pharaoh listen to me? The Israelites don't even listen to me, it must be because of my faltering lips. So Moses grew discouraged in his flesh and ability and began to disqualify himself. Now I'm not saying that this was a result of a spiritual attack, but it was out of his lack of confidence of self and God that he grew unconvinced that he was capable of doing something so significant. In these moments like the one that Moses was facing, God calls us to be faithful in pursuing the objective that He has put in our path. If Moses conceded to self-defeat, then I wonder if freedom would have come at the hands of another willing participant or if Israel would have been in bondage to Egypt forever.

ESTABLISHING YOUR AUTHORITY

*Luke 10:19*New International Version (NIV)*[19] I have given you authority to trample on snakes and scorpions and to overcome all the power of the enemy; nothing will harm you.*

Well that sums it up pretty quickly doesn't it? Jesus who was clothed in the Authority of the Father grants that same authority to His followers. When we don't realize that we have an authority that has a heavenly origin, then we will attempt to fight spiritual bombardments with human efforts. When the enemy comes against you, if you attempt to fight what is spiritual with the flesh you will surely lose. I am not trying to sound pessimistic or defeatist, but I am warning the body of Christ that if we do not attempt to make a relational connection with the Father that reveals our spiritual authority, then we are entering into a battle completely unarmed.

Commenters on this passage of scripture sight that Christ bestows this authority to the believer which was rightfully ours to begin with. This authority was at one point in time forfeited to the devil in the Garden of Eden, but won back in the wilderness by Jesus. This passage alludes to an authority that no matter how deadly the sting of the scorpion or the bite of the serpent, we will feel no effect because the power of God within us overcomes.

*2 Corinthians 10:4*New International Version (NIV)
[4] The weapons we fight with are not the weapons of the world. On the contrary, they have divine power to demolish strongholds.

Do you understand the level of power and authority that you have at your disposal? Do you understand that the authority that Christ fought for us to have is powerful enough to cast the enemy out of people, to heal the sick, to raise the dead, and to set the captive free? When I think about the idea of even coming near a snake or a scorpion, the idea makes me very uneasy. Why? Because creepy crawly things are scary! Right? I mean we give so much attention to the scary attributes of things and forget that we have more power than they do. I remember a professor of mine while I was in Seminary say "If Jesus is the Lion of Judah, and Satan is the imposter who poses as an angel of light, then Satan is the Lion roaring in the thicket who has no teeth". In other words, he looks big and bad but he is powerless compared to the children of God who carry a heavenly authority.

"All that Scripture teaches concerning devils aims at arousing us to take precaution against their stratagems and contrivances, and also to make us equip ourselves with those weapons which are strong and powerful enough to vanquish these most powerful foes." John Calvin Institutes of Christian Religion

According to Calvin it is not a suggestion but a mandate that we must as believers take up our authority to fight the present agents of evil in this world. A quick story about my experience with Spiritual warfare. When I was a young Christian I was a member of a local Church that was pastored by a man who is powerful in the Holy Spirit so I grew in my faith under the leadership of this man. While he would go on trips, he would ask me to house sit and watch his son who I also mentored. One night the Pastor's son and I were sitting out by the fire pit enjoying some good conversation when all of the sudden this sense came upon me that we were not alone. I quickly acknowledged to him that I sensed something in our presence and he quickly confirmed that he sensed the same. I told him that I would put out the fire pit as he went inside and I would go into battle with whatever was out there with me. I prayed, I fought, I beseeched the presence of the Holy Spirit to come and war alongside of me against this dark trespasser. When I felt like the presence had left, I filled the fire pit with water and went inside. As I turned to lock the door to my surprise the fire pit was a blaze…OK guess I'm not done was my response and I went out and fought for two more hours until the battle was won. Now my response could have been very different had I not known the authority that I carried in Christ.

EXERCISING YOUR AUTHORITY

So there are a few things that we can do that the enemy absolutely despises when it comes to taking up our authority.

1.   We stand on the truth of the Word of God.

Hebrews 4:12 New International Version (NIV)
12 For the word of God is alive and active. Sharper than any double-edged sword, it penetrates even to dividing soul and spirit, joints and marrow; it judges the thoughts and attitudes of the heart.

Because the Word of God is absolute truth, and the enemy is a liar, then when we come against his words with the truth of God's Word we will find ourselves able to overcome the enemy's strategy. This action of reading the Word and letting it penetrate your heart with the promises of God will begin to crumble the ground of deception that the enemy builds his base upon in your heart. In this passage in Hebrews, the fact that the Word of God judges the thoughts and attitudes of the heart leads me to believe that if there is any activity that isn't of the Lord then their must come a correction to the person which will lead to an eviction of ungodly activity.

Revelation 19:15 New International Version (NIV)
15 Coming out of his mouth is a sharp sword with which to strike down the nations. "He will rule them with an iron scepter." He treads the winepress of the fury of the wrath of God Almighty.

When the Heavenly warrior comes to battle the beast, neither the beast nor those who ascribe to his authority will be able to stand against the power of the Word of God almighty. The Sword in this passage symbolizes the judgement of God, and the scepter symbolizes His unbreakable eternal reign. If we allow the Word of the Lord to challenge and convict us in places where we have given authority to the enemy, then He will reign in our lives.

Remember when Jesus was in the wilderness during His forty day fast? What did satan attempt to do? He attempted to distort scripture in order to manipulate Jesus into forfeiting His destiny. Satan used scripture three times in an effort to sway Jesus' direction and three times Jesus retaliated by standing on the truth of the Word. Jesus obviously is going to know the Word of God better than satan, but this account goes to show us that when we become familiar with the truth of God's Word, then it becomes a weapon that we can use against the plans of the enemy.

2. We kneel for battle.

Matthew 26:41 New International Version (NIV)
[41] *"Watch and pray so that you will not fall into temptation. The spirit is willing, but the flesh is weak."*

Locking yourself away in prayer is like what I would imagine a battlefield briefing session would be like. It is a place where the troops receive strategy and warnings, they formulate their positions and they go over their rolls before they set out on a mission. The same with when we go before God to pray, I believe that God gives us wisdom, discernment, and strategy for how to deal with the enemy when he attacks. This Matthew 16 passage is reminding us that the enemy wants to get us in the place where we are the most vulnerable, but when we go before the Lord seeking strategy and wisdom, He will show us where there are any entry points that the enemy would try to attack, hence the weak flesh.

Prayer is also a source of strength to the tired and weary Christian. If we fail to acknowledge that our spiritual sustenance comes from taking our place at the banquet feast, then we run the risk of spiritual atrophy.

*Ephesians 3:16*New International Version (NIV)
[16] *I pray that out of his glorious riches he may strengthen you with power through his Spirit in your inner being,*

It is in prayer that our strength is renewed and restored. When we are disconnected, or separated from our heavenly Father, then we can be easily picked off by the enemy. I sometimes watch these shows on nature, and one of the most anxiety provoking moments in any show is when you see a herd of migrating deer or buffalo with babies being stalked by a predator. You hear the commentator talking about the calf who struggles to keep up with the herd and is outside of the protection of its parent, and then.......the predator makes its move. It's almost too hard to watch, but this is also how the enemy works, when you are spiritually disconnected the enemy will attempt to pick you off because you have stepped away from the covering of the herd.

When we pray we seek direction, and covering. We stop trying to fight the enemy in our own flesh and enter into our spiritual power with the Holy Spirit.

*Ephesians 6:12*New International Version (NIV)
12 For our struggle is not against flesh and blood, but against the rulers, against the authorities, against the powers of this dark world and against the spiritual forces of evil in the heavenly realms.

We don't fight spirit with flesh but with spirit, Matthew tells us that the flesh is weak so why battle in it. Put on then the spirit and be clothed in the authority of God almighty to battle the forces of evil.

3. Worship is Warship

The way that you respond to the attack will dictate whether or not he will be victorious over you or whether you will defeat his advances. When we know that with God we are victorious over the plans of the enemy, we will engage our warfare with praise. This act of praise averts the advancement of the enemy. One of the tactics of Satan is to break down your will and if he is successful in that, you will find it very difficult to combat his advances. I retold a story a couple of chapters ago about a time when I combatted a spiritual attack with praise. The result was a complete break in the atmosphere where the enemy attempted to control, the Holy Spirit came in a regained the territory of my heart and mind.

Acts 16:24-26New International Version (NIV)
24 When he received these orders, he put them in the inner cell and fastened their feet in the stocks.

25 About midnight Paul and Silas were praying and singing hymns to God, and the other prisoners were listening to them. 26 Suddenly there was such a violent earthquake that the foundations of the prison were shaken. At once all the prison doors flew open, and everyone's chains came loose.

Paul and Silas weren't in the most desirable situation, but what they didn't allow their predicament to do was dictate how they engaged God and contended for His promises. It's easy to accept your fate as a prisoner who has been convicted of a crime, but when your crime is advancing the kingdom of God then you are less willing to accept this imprisonment. The petitions of Paul and Silas called for the righteous judge to hand pass down an acquittal which resulted in their release from prison. When we are under spiritual attack, the enemy attempts to arrest us for crimes committed against the kingdom of darkness but ultimately he has no warrant. When we go before God with praise and supplication knowing that we are not deserving of this charge, he shakes the grounds of false accusation from the enemy and sets us free.

I am not afraid of the devil. He can't handle the one whom I joined"
A.W. Tozer

CHAPTER

SIX

POWERFULLY MEEK

As men and women of Jesus Christ, we are called to be in a constant operational flow of the Holy Spirit. Let me explain to you what I mean by this… the Holy Spirit is not episodic! We need to be clothed or filled with the Holy Spirit continually. Paul admonishes the Church in Ephesus to be *continually* filled with the Holy Spirit. So what does that look like for the believer? That means that daily we need to walk in the power, authority, and glory of the Holy Spirit. When we walk in the constant presence of the Holy Spirit, then we are more open and free to allow the power and presence of God to influence us. Moses explained this experience when he would enter into the presence of God in the tabernacle. The account states that when Moses went before God in prayer with a spirit of meekness God promised that His presence would go before him and His glory would surround him. The definition of meekness is "to be easily imposed upon". Now for some of us we might look at this definition and think it to be a complete intrusion of personal space, but when it comes to our relationship with God it equates to anointing and empowerment for the service of God.

I believe that the only reason why Moses was able to meet face to face with God on the mountain at Sinai and why God was so receptive to Moses was because of his position of availability and willingness before God. Meekness assumes a posture that shouts to the heavens "here I am Lord send me" and then responds with an unhesitant "amen" at the reception of the command. To quote J. Hector Fezandie, "With great power comes great responsibility". Meekness before God calls upon a divine response which results in an outpouring of Holy Spirit power, with the occurrence of this outpouring it is the responsibility of the anointed and spiritually saturated to dispense that which was poured out upon them. Meekness is not a passive state, it's an active presence. Moses entered the presence of God and then went and executed his orders to the Israelites. He sought the presence of the Lord, received his mandate, was clothed in His glory, and was released to minister.

This is the same way that the baptism of the Holy Spirit works for the believer. The man or woman who makes room in their heart for Jesus and takes on the posture of meekness is showered by the soul drenching overflow of the Holy Spirit and then is called to go out and operate.

WHAT IS THE BAPTISM OF THE HOLY SPIRIT?

First if we are going to grasp the understanding of the baptism of the Holy Spirit we have to know what it is and what it isn't.

1. The baptism of the Holy Spirit is the successor of the Baptism of repentance. John states in Matthew 3:11 "*I baptize you with water for repentance, but he who is coming after me is mightier than I...He will baptize you with the Holy Spirit and with fire.*" There is a preceding requirement for the baptism of the Holy Spirit and that is the "believer's baptism"

2. The baptism of repentance is necessary for anyone who desires the baptism of the Holy Spirit.

    ### Acts 1:4-5 NIV
    Repent, and be baptized for the forgiveness of your sins; and you shall <u>receive</u> the gift of the Holy Spirit.

    Notice the conditional language that is used here, you do this...and you will get this... Now you might be thinking that's unfair, but I believe that the reason behind this prerequisite is that someone who truly hasn't gone through the first baptism will never be able to give the glory and honor of the manifest gifts to God. The baptism of repentance is entered into with a humble and contrite heart, a heart that is dedicated to the refinement and discipline of the Lord and His service. A heart that has not been offered in this manner will only glorify itself whenever the Holy Spirit moves.

3. The Holy Spirit work at conversion is not the same as the Holy Spirit work at the second baptism. The role of the Holy Spirit at conversion draws the new believer to an acknowledgment that Jesus Christ is Lord, it enlightens the believer to scripture, sin, and seals them for salvation. The Holy Spirit at the second baptism empowers the believer to activate and operate in the "charismatic" gifts ie. tongues, prophecy, words of wisdom and knowledge, healing, deliverance etc.

4. The baptism of the Holy Spirit is a promise not a requirement.

Acts 2:39New International Version (NIV)

39 The promise is for you and your children and for all who are far off—for all whom the Lord our God will call."

I wouldn't want to attempt to operate in my Christian walk knowing that there is an opportunity to have such a powerful offering made for me to reflect and manifest the glory of the living God. I believe that a refusal of this offer is to withhold the kingdom from the world, since we are called to be the holders of the light of Christ, we should not place any cover over it that would leave people in a state of utter darkness.

The way that I see the baptism of the Holy Spirit in the progress of the believer is as follows: I like to draw the analogy of the rebuilding of the temple in Jerusalem after its destruction by the Babylonians. When we come before God we are the ruins of God's original creation, we are broken, a shell of what God made us to be. When we come to God He rebuilds us, no longer a pile of rubble broken by the world but a masterpiece that reflects the glory of our rebuilder. But now that we have gone through a rebuilding process there is still the process of furnishing the temple with things that honor and magnify God, the baptism of the Holy Spirit is the adornment of the temple. It is easy to go through the Christian life or life in general looking the part but not being an activated believer. Your identity from the beginning was never to just look like a Christian, it was to reflect Jesus and the only way we will reflect Jesus in His fullest is when we enter into the baptism of the Holy Spirit.

CLOTHED IN POWER AND RIGHTEOUSNESS

Luke 24:49 New International Version (NIV)

49 I am going to send you what my Father has promised; but stay in the city until you have been clothed with power from on high."

The gifts of the Holy Spirit given to the Spirit clothed believer are nothing short of true power. It is by the baptism of the Holy Spirit that God touches the lives of others through His willing servant. The account of the events at pentecost recounts a group of believers awaiting the foretold arrival of the Spirit of God. Now what we don't read in the account of pentecost is that the disciples that were present just sat around discussing the events of the day reasoning and rationalizing what just happened, or that they remained together sharing the gifts only among themselves. What we see is a body of believers so captivated and ignited by the glorious power of Christ that they couldn't remain in the upper room but needed to enter the streets bringing the power to the people.

When we are Baptized in the Holy Spirit, we are clothed in the power of Jesus Christ, just like the garment that Jesus wore that the bleeding woman touched and was healed, we now are adorned by that garment when the Holy Spirit is upon us. After pentecost we have accounts of the disciples going out in power, healing the sick and lame, and bringing the unbeliever to life giving faith.

Acts 3:6-10New International Version (NIV)

6 Then Peter said, "Silver or gold I do not have, but what I do have I give you. In the name of Jesus Christ of Nazareth, walk." 7 Taking him by the right hand, he helped him up, and instantly the man's feet and ankles became strong. 8 He jumped to his feet and began to walk. Then he went with them into the temple courts, walking and jumping, and praising God. 9 When all the people saw him walking and praising God, 10 they recognized him as the same man who used to sit begging at the temple gate called Beautiful, and they were filled with wonder and amazement at what had happened to him.

Notice the point of contact...Peter took him by the right hand and lifted him to his once powerless feet and the man became able to walk. Peter extended the hand of healing, salvation, deliverance and redemption. At the moment of healing, the man praised God because he recognized the power that he came in contact with was not Peter, it was

Jesus. When we allow the Holy Spirit to cloth us in power, the people that are impacted by our mission will know the maker of the garment we wear and they will praise Jesus.

Now while the clothing of the Holy Spirit makes the believer a greater reflection of their savior, it also re establishes the appearance and identity of the Church. When the individual operates in the power of the Spirit, then they will in turn impact other individuals. When a Church is operating in the power of the Holy Spirit then towns, cities, and countries can experience that power through the climate of Revival that is cultivated in those bodies of worship.

Acts 2:42–47 New International Version (NIV)

The Fellowship of the Believers

42 They devoted themselves to the apostles' teaching and to fellowship, to the breaking of bread and to prayer. 43 Everyone was filled with awe at the many wonders and signs performed by the apostles. 44 All the believers were together and had everything in common. 45 They sold property and possessions to give to anyone who had need. 46 Every day they continued to meet together in the temple courts. They broke bread in their homes and ate together with glad and sincere hearts, 47 praising God and enjoying the favor of all the people. And the Lord added to their number daily those who were being saved.

The contagion of the Holy Spirit drew those in the impact radius of the disciples into the fellowship of believers. When the Church is aligned in the power of the Holy Spirit together, then Revival has a foundation to rest on and awakening becomes a natural bi-product of the presence of the Holy Spirit that dwells in the community of a united Church. I remember when I was a volunteer leader for Younglife for many years, the slogan that we used was "you were made for this". Such a simple yet powerfully true statement to make us aware that we were made to be a powerful example of Jesus Christ, His goodness in our life, His grace, His mercy, His power, His authority, and to be not a presentation but an encounter where people engage with Jesus through us.

Isaiah 61:10 New International Version (NIV)

10 *I delight greatly in the Lord;*
my soul rejoices in my God.
For he has clothed me with garments of salvation
and arrayed me in a robe of his righteousness,
as a bridegroom adorns his head like a priest,
and as a bride adorns herself with her jewels.

I heard someone cite this quote *"becoming a Christian is the easiest decision you can make but the hardest thing you will ever do"*. No truer words have been spoken, when I look at the menu of what Jesus has to offer us, and the opportunities afforded us when we present Him with a heart surrendered and a willingness of self submitted it is easy to say YES!!!. But there we only begin on the journey of daily seeking the righteousness of our Lord which calls for us to cast off all self righteousness and to cast off the old self which belongs to our former manner of life and to start living with a transformed mind that is daily focused on the Lord and His ways.

In the previous chapter we spoke about Spiritual attack and warfare, one of the elements of warfare is to torpedo the authority and power of the Holy Spirit in you by distorting the righteousness of God in you and giving you over to a depraved mind. I have seen it many times, a wonderfully powerful man or woman of God taken out completely because they had a moment when they let down there defenses and allowed the enemy a foothold. When we are operating in the power of God, we must daily clothe ourselves in HIs righteousness. The enemy prowls like a roaring lion waiting to devour any who are not situationally aware.

Ephesians 6:10–20 New International Version (NIV)

The Armor of God

10 *Finally, be strong in the Lord and in his mighty power.* **11** *Put on the full armor of God, so that you can take your stand against the devil's schemes.* **12** *For our struggle is not against flesh and blood, but against the rulers, against the authorities, against the powers of this dark world and against the spiritual forces of evil in the heavenly realms.* **13** *Therefore put on the full armor of God, so that when the day of evil comes, you may be able to stand your ground, and after you have done everything, to stand.* **14** *Stand firm then, with the belt of truth buckled around your waist, with the breastplate of righteousness in place,* **15** *and with your feet fitted with the readiness that comes from the gospel of peace.* **16** *In addition to all this, take up the shield of faith, with which you can extinguish all the flaming arrows of the evil one.* **17** *Take the helmet of salvation and the sword of the Spirit, which is the word of God.*

18 *And pray in the Spirit on all occasions with all kinds of prayers and requests. With this in mind, be alert and always keep on praying for all the Lord's people.* **19** *Pray also for me, that whenever*

*I speak, words may be given me so that I will fearlessly make known the mystery of the gospel, **20** for which I am an ambassador in chains. Pray that I may declare it fearlessly, as I should.*

> When I wake every morning this is my prayer: "Lord today i pray that I would be supported in the truth of your Holy Word, that your righteousness would guard my heart, that my feet would go wherever you take me on today's journey, that i would have an impenetrable faith that defends my heart from the lies of the enemy, that my thoughts would be filled with heavenly visions, and that your Word would be my defense".

We are called to be warriors of heaven, not casualties of the things of this world. While we are all called to operate in the authority and power of Christ, it is equally if not more critical to remain in His righteousness. that means our thoughts must be pure, our eyes must abstain from anything that is unclean and our words and actions must be exalting of our Lord. Think about this...a glass of water that is ninety nine percent pure but contains one percent contamination can still offer a lethal dose of whatever toxin is in it. So we need to make sure that we allow God to purify us every day, to make sure there is no contaminant that could poison us or those who we are called to minister to.

FINAL THOUGHTS

The concept of being a Free Spirit is to become the man and woman of Christ that you were designed to be. The Holy Spirit in you wants to be granted the permission to permeate every area of your life and to empower you to do the greater works. The world gives us a false perception of reality and puts the cork on the bottle trapping the Holy Spirit from being released in your life. A discipline of reminding ourselves that we might live in the world but we are certainly not of it, will set us free from the bondage of a false reality and lights the fuse of the Holy Spirit to explode in your life. This is a time of great awakening, I believe that God is calling all of us to wake up! open our eyes! and see what the Lord is doing in our midst. It is time for all of us to turn up the lights in our lives and in the world, to call the darkness into light and to bring fresh revelation to a fallen world through the testimony that we bear.

The hardest thing about this journey is allowing yourself to be completely honest and open with yourself and with God. If you are willing to let this book challenge you I believe that you will experience a freedom that you have never had in your life. Don't forget, we are a work in progress. Just because you feel as though you unloaded a whole bunch of stuff doesn't mean that somewhere on the journey of life you won't pick up other things that you may need to surrender. This is not a destination, it's an adventure with Jesus. I would encourage you after reading this book and making it a meditation for your life to spend time with a Pastor who can help you to continue to navigate your new found freedom and revelation of self and Christ. If you are not in a Church I encourage you to find a Bible believing Church filled with the Holy Spirit to help you on your journey. We aren't meant to travel this journey alone, but alongside of brothers and sisters in Christ and with wise counsel from a Pastor.

I pray that you now live in the brightest of lights, Jesus, the Lord and Savior of the world who desires good things for your life and wants to live in intimacy with you forever. Amen

2 Corinthians 3:17 New International Version (NIV)

17 Now the Lord is the Spirit, and where the Spirit of the Lord is, there is freedom.

WORKS CITED

Packer, J.I. <u>Knowing God</u>; Intervarsity press 1973
    Taken from <u>A Quest for Godliness</u> by J.I. Packer, © 1994,
    pp. 116. Used by permission of Crossway, a publishing
    ministry of Good News Publishers, Wheaton, IL 60187,
    www.crossway.org.

Tozer, A.W. <u>The Counselor</u>; Wingspread Publishers, Camp
hill PA. 2009

Johnson, Bill <u>Hosting the presence</u>; Destiny images,
Shippensburg PA. 2012

LeStrange, Ryan <u>Overcoming Spiritual attack</u>; Charisma
House, Lake Mary Fla. 2016

Calvin, John <u>Institutes of Christian Religion</u>; Hendrickson
Pub. 2007

All quoted Scriptures are from the NIV 1984 edition
published by Hendrickson publishing and the International
Bible Society 2005. Isbn 1-56563-639-2

Printed in the United States
By Bookmasters